Why You Should Not Join The U.S. Military

Published by Travis Haan

Copyright 2015 by Travis Haan

ISBN 9781520692968

TABLE OF CONTENTS

1. Introduction

2. Nine Reasons Not To Join The United States Military

3. You Can Support The UCMJ Or The Troops But Not Both

4. Four Reasons American Troops Are As Much Victims As They Are Heroes

5. The Military Is A Cult

6. How And Why Basic Training Brainwashes Recruits

7. The Parallels Between The Stanford Prison Experiment and Tech School

8. An Overdue Critique Of The Military Caste System

9. Quantifying The Heroism Of Troops

10. A Veteran's "State Of The Troops" Address On The 10th Anniversary of September 11th

11. An Open Letter To The United States Military

1. INTRODUCTION

My name is Travis Haan, and I enlisted in the U.S. Air Force in the year 2000 at the age of 20. I served for seven years as a 3C0X1 (Communications computer systems operator). My duties included trouble shooting network outages, repairing and programming network switches and routers, maintaining computer servers and performing basic help desk support. In chronological order, I was stationed at Lackland, Texas, Keesler Mississipi, Aviano Italy, Sembach, Germany, Ali Al Salem, Kuwait, Kunia, Hawaii and Hickam, Hawaii.

In tech school at Keesler I volunteered to serve as a student leader aka "green rope." Throughout my military career I received many squadron coins, letters of appreciation and was regularly put in positions of authority above my pay grade. The highest rank I held was rank was E-5 (Staff Sergeant). In 2007 the 3C0X1 career field was downsized, and I was offered the opportunity to volunteer to separate early with an honorable discharge. I accepted the offer and separated a year and half before the end of my contract.

I'll be honest. I didn't join for patriotism, honor or tradition. I volunteered because I was poor, and the military was the quickest, surest way for me to get a good job and a good education. As I progressed through basic training and tech school I asked hundreds of my peers why they joined, and almost all of them said they joined for the same reasons. Though we started out suburban mercenaries, by the time we graduated basic training we were proud to be a part of the military family. I sincerely would have killed or died to support America's mission. For the first few years of my enlistment I slept soundly, confident in the knowledge that I was making the world a better place. I even reenlisted to serve my country longer and enjoy all the perks of being in the military.

I separated early and gave up free medical care, free housing, guaranteed retirement pay and free travel. I was stationed in Hawaii at the time, and I gladly gave up the opportunity to live there for another year and a half, because over the course of my enlistment I witnessed such flaws in the military system so severe that I came to believe the cost/benefit analysis of serving in the military didn't added up. If I knew at age of twenty, what I know now, I would never have joined the military.

I share my reasons with you knowing that it will upset many active duty troops and veterans. I don't do this lightly. I'm not just whining because I didn't like my job or people weren't nice enough to me. Nor is the issue that the military just wasn't right for me. My complaints aren't subjective. I firmly believe that even people who love being in the military should boycott reenlisting to protest the unethical ways the military treats its troops, fights its wars and serves the interests of the financial elite over the needs of the poor.

This book isn't an attack on the troops who continue to serve, and the call to action it raises isn't to abolish the military. It's a sober, heavy-hearted plea for all of us to reexamine the military system and correct its flaws.

I wrote my critique of the military in the form of ten essays, which I posted on my website, TheWiseSloth.com over the past six years. Since then I've received hundreds of comments and E-mails from active duty troops and veterans thanking for me putting their experiences into words. I've also received a lot of negative feedback from active duty troops and veterans who vehemently disagree with my interpretation of the military.

Even if you disagree with me, just know that I'm not a lone voice. You're disagreeing with thousands of other men and women who served proudly but lost their faith for the same reasons.

Before the book beings, I'd like to address seven of the most common complaints I've received from readers:

Common criticisms of this essay:

1. The military is not a cult! I served in the military and never knew anyone who was brainwashed!

There's no point arguing whether or not the military is a cult without referencing a checklist of cult practices. Read any book on cults and brainwashing techniques. The more you know about cults, brainwashing techniques and military culture, the more obvious it will be that the military is deliberately designed using every unethical mind control technique used by cults.

2. You were in the Air Force and never saw combat. So you don't know what you're talking about.

You can say I'm not a hero because I never saw combat, and I won't argue with that. But my role in the military has no bearing on whether or not the military is a cult. It has no bearing on the fact that the United States government has consistently eliminated more and more rights of its citizens, spied on its citizens, persecuted whistle blowers, knowingly killed civilians and committed deliberate war crimes and crimes against humanity. These are all facts that can be verified by anyone, even people who never served in the military or saw combat at all.

I never experienced battle in the military. So I can't speak with authority on combat. All of my experiences in the military involved traveling around bases, installing and repairing infrastructure, analyzing the needs of every organization, and networking with their chain of command. My job required me to understand the internal workings of the military. On that topic I feel like I can speak with some authority.

3. You were probably just a dirt bag Airman who wasn't cut out for the military, and that's why you're bitter and wrong about everything.

I wasn't always the most gung-ho super troop, but for the most part, I was a model troop. So if you're going to base the truth of my words on the quality of my character then you should believe what I have to say about the United States military. But you don't have to take my word on anything. Do your own research, and you'll find everything I've said here is true, and it still would be even if I was a dirt bag Airman, which I wasn't.

4. All the questionable training methods and rules the military uses are necessary to weed out the weak and prepare the strong for war. At worst, it's a necessary evil, but it keeps you free. So enjoy your self-righteous freedom to whine on the internet while real men keep you safe.

No sane person would charge a beach under heavy gunfire, but somebody theoretically has to do it. So the military takes sane civilians and reprograms their minds to turn them into zealous, suicidal killers, and it does this using the exact same brainwashing techniques used by death cults. This is illegal to do to anyone else, and it's still unethical when the U.S. government does it legally.

I can accept that it requires extreme training techniques to prepare soldiers for the extreme stresses of war. What I can't accept is the military lying to recruits, telling them basic training will turn them into self-actualized adults, when it's specifically designed to break their sanity and take away their identity and free will. The problem here isn't that I need to shut up and stop being a pussy. At the very least, the problem here is that the U.S. military should be more transparent.

The argument that misleading and brainwashing volunteers is a necessary evil that has to take place in order to keep the rest of the American population free doesn't apply when the American government keeps taking away its citizens' freedom and privacy. Worse than that, it keeps passing more laws that make it harder for the poor to have a decent quality of life. If Americans were truly free, they would have the freedom to decide if they want their tax dollars spent on brainwashing soldiers or endless wars, but Americans don't have that choice. They have to pay their taxes and fund the industrial war complex or go to jail. If they protest against it, they'll be spied on, and if their protest is too successful, they'll go to jail. People are free to criticize the government some times in some ways, but journalists who report criminal activity committed by the American government are routinely jailed. That's not freedom of speech. That's leeway of speech.

The problem isn't that I don't appreciate the sacrifices soldiers have made to protect my freedoms. The problem is that my freedoms are being whittled away despite the sacrifices of soldiers. If you support the troops, then you shouldn't get mad at me for pointing out that the American government is systemically corrupt and manipulates its soldiers into believing they're defending freedom when they're really defending corruption. If you support the troops, then get mad at the government that's making a mockery of its soldiers' sacrifices.

5. I was in the military, and I enjoyed it. Plus I got paid well and learned valuable job skills. Hence, the military is good.

The fact that you enjoyed the military and got a lot out of it doesn't change the fact that the military is a cult that treats its own troops in ways that are hands-down illegal to treat anyone else. The benefits any troops do get out of the military are still stained with the shame of the rights American citizens have lost and the blood of the civilians the American government has killed.

6. Anyone who criticizes the military is a pussy.

Calling someone you don't agree with a pussy isn't an argument. It's a gut reaction. The topic of how the military industrial complex manipulates and uses the troops is too important to end with a gut reaction. If there's any chance that anything I say here is true, it deserves serious, soul-searching thought. Refusing to consider opposing points of view isn't brave or mature, and it doesn't do the people whose freedoms you think you're killing and dying for any favors.

7. I can't believe what a crazy conspiracy theorist nut this author is. His ideas are unbelievably wacko.

As I said earlier, I've received hundreds of comments and E-mails from veterans and active duty service members thanking me for articulating what they've been thinking but couldn't say. It should worry you how so many people could come up with the exact same conspiracy theories. These ideas aren't conspiracy theories. They're the elephant in the room.

2. NINE REASONS NOT TO JOIN THE UNITED STATES MILITARY

1. The military is a death cult that brainwashes you.

The military is painstakingly designed around the cult model, and the two biggest red flags that the military is a cult are its unethical indoctrination process and totalitarian, pyramid shaped caste system. Other warning signs are the use of an inside language, in-group symbols, rituals, in-group socializing, constantly telling you that the military is your family, convincing you that military history is your history and other tactics that convince you to base your identity and purpose in life primarily on the military. Individually these practices aren't necessarily sinister, but the military goes to extreme lengths to use every trick in the book every day to convince its members to base their identity on the in-group and devote their life to it. That's what cults do, and the military does it better than anyone.

2. You'll kill and possibly die to defend the very ideals you swore to fight against.

There's no country in the world that wants to take away America's freedoms. The only people in the world who want to take away Americans' freedoms are the very politicians who every active duty soldier swears an oath of allegiance to, and America's leaders have been very successful at taking away Americans' freedoms, especially since September 11th, 2001.

America is no longer the land of the free, and it's also no longer a representative democracy. It's a corportocracy controlled by the rich, for the rich. America doesn't even defend democracy abroad. America is the only country actively toppling democracies. Look that up. It's not a conspiracy. It's common knowledge.

If you join the United States military you won't fight for truth, justice or freedom. You'll fight for a government that crushes public dissent and locks up more people than any other country in the world in a for-profit prison system that uses inmates as slave labor. You won't fight for peace. You'll fight for a country that commits human rights violations, spies on its own citizens and locks up whistle blowers while protecting war criminals. You'll fight for a country that destabilizes weaker countries to allow multinational businesses to fleece them out of their natural resources and outsource jobs to their sweatshops. The American military might fight against terrorism, but it also engages in terrorism and creates more terrorists every time it kills innocent civilians, which is almost every month.

There are no serious foreign threats to America's way of life. Possibly the biggest threat to the average American's quality of life is America's own industrial war complex, which directs billions of tax dollars every year to killing peasants while America's schools crumble from lack of funding.

If you support America's military mission, you won't make the world a better place. In the end, your noble sacrifices will make the world a worse place, but don't take my word for it. If you want to know what America's military stands for, ask the people of Diego Garcia.

3. The military cares about you the same way a slave owner cares about his slaves.

The military will convince you to love it so much you'll get military tattoos, wear military-themed civilian clothing and yell at anyone who criticizes the military, but the military doesn't return that loyalty. Sure, the military gives its troops a lot of perks and bonuses, but like all other cults, the pampering stops the second you start questioning the organization. If you don't drink the Kool-Aid you'll get thrown out in the streets for "failure to conform."

If you breach the military's puritanical code of ethics the military won't hesitate to throw the book at you as hard as possible to make an example of you. The military also loves group punishments. Sooner or later you'll be punished for something someone else did. Your superiors won't care that it's unfair. Group punishment dehumanizes you, conditions you to police your peers and reinforces the idea that higher ranking personnel wield total and unquestionable power over you. It's a powerful psychological tool to keep you obedient and submissive. The military has a long history of using its troops to test medicines and chemicals on. The brainwashing techniques used in basic training and tied into the military's culture of "customs and courtesies" disregard your right to define your own identity and purpose in life. You're just a number to the military, and it only cares about you to the extent that you're useful to it.

4. You'll lose almost all of your civil rights.

You'll lose the right to free speech, the right to assembly (at least, the right to assemble with any group that opposes the agenda of the military). You'll lose the right to work a second job at any business the military disagrees with. You'll lose the right to enter businesses that the military disagrees with. You'll lose the right to self-determination. You won't be able to quit your job when you've reached the point where you hate it or disagree with it. Your home life will affect your work life. You can be demoted or even lose your job for legal trouble you get into on your private time. There will be limits to what kinds of tattoos you can get and where you can get them. There will be limits to what kind of piercings you can get and even what kind of civilian clothing you can wear on base. You can't even make a private sex tape. You can theoretically go to jail for not doing a jumping jack, not buttoning your shirt, talking back to your boss, quitting your job, not taking your hat off when you go inside, not saluting the flag or walking on the grass. You can even get charged with destruction of government property for getting a sunburn on your day off.

Just to be safe, Article 134 of the Uniform Code of Military Justice that says pretty much anything you do can be considered against the law; someone in your chain of command just has to say that something you did was bad, and that makes it against the rules. See for yourself:

"Though not specifically mentioned in this chapter, all disorders and neglects to the prejudice of good order and discipline in the armed forces, all conduct of a nature to bring discredit upon the armed forces, and crimes and offenses not capital, of which persons subject to this chapter may be guilty, shall be taken cognizance of by a general, special, or summary court-martial, according to the nature and degree of the offense, and shall be punished at the discretion of that court."

You'll lose many more rights listed in the Uniform Code of Military Justice that nobody will go out of their way to tell you about until after you've signed your soul away. And if you ever complain you'll be told, "You knew exactly what you were getting into when you signed up."

Individually, some of these points may seem trivial to you, but when you add them all up, the end result is that the government owns you completely. If you only want to do whatever the government allows you to, then you might not even notice your own loss of freedom and dignity. But if you do value your rights and freedom, and if you realize that the government you're fighting for is holding a metaphorical gun to your head 24 hours a day, 365 days a year, you might start feeling claustrophobic 24 hours a day, 365 days a year. Once you realize that you're not fighting for anyone else's freedoms except the robber barons who own your corrupt politicians, the cost/benefit analysis of giving up your rights to a death cult that doesn't care about you ceases to add up.

5. Your self-worth will become based on rank.

When you go through basic training you'll be told that upon graduation you'll become an adult. In fact, you'll become more than an adult. You'll become a member of the elite echelon of society. Your maturity and responsibility will make you superior to the petty, selfish, undisciplined civilian herd.

However, the reality of life in the military does not reflect the propaganda you'll be fed in basic training. The reality of your day to day life is comparable to what you experienced in high school. Everyone in the ranks between E-1 to E-4 are treated like high school students. The ranks of E-5 and E-6 are treated like teachers, and E-7 to E-9 are treated like school administrators.

When you wear the bottom four ranks you'll be treated like children. Your superiors will look down on you, talk down to you, bully you and rub their rank in your face. You'll be made to do menial chores and do the bulk of the work. You'll be punished severely for any and every infraction possible. You'll even be punished for things you didn't do wrong, and you'll have very little recourse to fight this, because your worth is based on your rank, and your rank is that of a peon. When you reach the middle tier ranks you'll finally be treated like a human being. Your job will mainly involve training the lower ranks and managing paperwork. You'll be less accountable for your actions and will have comfortable leeway to bend the rules. When you reach the top tiers of the enlisted pyramid you'll become a figure head. You'll spend most of your days doing paperwork and giving speeches. Since there are very few people above you to hold you accountable, and all of those people are in your club, you'll be almost unaccountable for your actions. You'll have to seriously screw up to get in trouble.

The power dynamic between the officer corps and the enlisted corps is comparable to slave owners and slaves. The slave owners are treated like gods and literally dine on golden plates under golden chandeliers. They have total power over the lower class and destroy their underlings' lives with the snap of a finger. They're trained to believe in their superiority and wear their arrogance on their sleeves. They are less accountable for their actions. They'll get in far less trouble for committing the same crimes as enlisted troops if they get in trouble at all. Being an officer is a very good life to have... and a very immoral one. It is an obsolete class structure that degrades the value of the lives of the human beings who wear enlisted ranks and directly contradicts the ideal of human equality.

This is a strange way to live, but other than being degrading to the lowest ranking troops, it might not seem like a compelling reason not to join the military. What new recruits need to be aware of is that after you've been indoctrinated to base your identity on your rank, that indoctrination doesn't always go away after you leave the military. If you spend 4 years as a low ranking enlisted troop and then separate, you're likely to go back out into the real world with a subservient mindset. But If you spend 4 years as an officer and then separate, you're likely to go back out into the real world believing the human population is divided into those who deserve to be obeyed/served and those who deserve to obey/serve, and you're one of the gods among men who deserve to be obeyed and served. These delusions of grandeur may feel empowering, but they're indoctrinated insanity, and leaders who think this way tend to act more like dictators than mentors.

6. The benefits aren't as good as you think.

Theoretically you're supposed to get preference when applying for federal jobs. Sometimes you do, and sometimes you don't. For all the other jobs out there, military experience can sometimes hurt your chances of getting a job because many civilians see veterans as dumb grunts who can't think for themselves. Veterans can potentially suffer the irrational stigma that they're unstable killers suffering from PTSD.

You won't get much if any VA medical help unless you were injured while in the military or you retired through the military. Even then, the VA system is famous for being a nightmare. Don't take my word for it. Visit a VA hospital before you join the military and see what you're signing up for.

You can retire in 20 years, but a large portion of your paychecks in the military are made up of housing pay, Cost of living adjustments and other side benefits that you don't pay taxes on. This looks great at the time, but your retirement pay is based on your taxable income. For enlisted troops this is only enough to live well on in the Philippines.

The MGI Bill has finally become usable, and it's a really good deal. The VA will also vouch for the down payment on your house, which is a really, really good deal. But no matter how good the monetary benefits of joining the military are, it's still all blood money.

7. Life in the military sucks...but don't take my word for it.

I'm sorry that it has come to this- A soldier's last words:

http://gawker.com/i-am-sorry-that-it-has-come-to-this-a-soldiers-last-534538357

One of many news reports about suicide in the military:

http://abcnews.go.com/blogs/politics/2011/11/new-report-military-losing-the-battle-against-suicide/

A special report/feature about suicides by a military newspaper:

http://www.stripes.com/news/special-reports/suicide-in-the-military

Article about veterans struggling to get help for post-traumatic stress disorder:

http://globalresearch.ca/index.php?context=va&aid=19633

A documentary about rape in the military:

http://invisiblewarmovie.com/

A military chat forum discussing how common sexual harassment is in the military:

http://www.reddit.com/r/AskReddit/comments/2or2yg/serious females_in_military_how_common_is_sexual/

A blog about the serious flaws in the Marine Corps, written by Marine veterans:

http://ihatetheusmc.com/

The most gruesome moments in the CIA torture report about Guantanamo Bay:

http://www.thedailybeast.com/articles/2014/12/09/the-most-gruesome-moments-in-the-cia-torture-report.html?

A good summary of what American soldiers are sent to fight for:

http://www.bostonreview.net/us/war-betrayal-chris-hedges

A rant by an Army vet about how he lost faith in America's military mission:

http://upriser.com/posts/you-grow-up-wanting-to-be-luke-skywalker-then-realize-you-ve-become-a-stormtrooper-for-the-empire

A documentary about U.S. soldiers killing civilians:

https://www.youtube.com/watch?v=eEMKwY1vF_8

8. Military culture is devolving into a maniacally politically correct, anal-retentive bureaucratic snow flake office Hell.

I'll explain what life is like in the Air Force, and you can just subtract a few degrees for each of the other branches: Cussing at all is frowned up, and in a lot of offices it's banned. The only kind of music you can listen to at work are Pop and Christian. You can't make crude jokes. You can be court martialed for sexual harassment for saying the word "vagina." There was a public service announcement commercial that ran on the

Armed Forces Television Network at my first duty station that said, "You don't have to do anything to be guilty of sexual harassment." Literally. It literally said that. You can't smoke anywhere but at isolated, designated smoking areas, and you can't smoke at all on some bases. You can't put your hands in your pockets. You can't walk and talk on your cell phone. You can't walk on the grass. You have to wear standard-issue reflective clothing when walking around at night. You'll get yelled at for wearing any article of civilian clothing on base that you wouldn't wear to church. You generally have to act like Ned Flanders or you'll get yelled at for being unprofessional... and you can theoretically go to jail and have the rest of your life destroyed with a dishonorable discharge if you don't.

There is some validity to these rules, but when you add all of them up (and the many others not mentioned) and continue to make more and more rules that force everyone to act like a neutered youth pastors, you create an environment that's less like the adventure advertised on recruiting commercials and more like the embodiment of everything the movie "Office Space" was satirizing.

People who can't conform to that standard end up leaving the military willingly or unwillingly. Those who act the most whitewashed and sanitized rise to the top. So that's who you work for, and that's who you work with. That's the environment you eat, sleep and breathe in. If the puritanical lifestyle appeals to you, and you don't mind being complicit in the deaths of hundreds of civilians every year then join the Air Force.

9. You'll be indoctrinated with battered person syndrome.

"When Battered Person Syndrome (BPS) manifests as PTSD, it consists of the following symptoms:

Re-experiencing the battering as if it were recurring even when it is not

Attempts to avoid the psychological impact of battering by avoiding activities, people, and emotions

Hyperarousal or hypervigilance

Disrupted interpersonal relationships

Body image distortion or other somatic concerns

Sexuality and intimacy issues.

Additionally, repeated cycles of violence and reconciliation can result in the following beliefs and attitudes:

The abused thinks that the violence was his or her fault.

The abused has an inability to place the responsibility for the violence elsewhere.

The abused fears for his/her life and/or the lives of his/her children (if present).

The abused has an irrational belief that the abuser is omnipresent and omniscient.

The syndrome develops in response to a three-stage cycle found in domestic violence situations. First, tension builds in the relationship. Second, the abusive partner releases tension via violence while blaming the victim for having caused the violence. Third, the violent partner makes gestures of contrition. However, the partner does not find solutions to avoid another phase of tension building and release so the cycle repeats. The repetition of the violence despite the abuser's attempts to "make nice" results in the abused partner feeling at fault for not preventing a repeat cycle of violence. However, since the victim is not at fault and the violence is internally driven by the abuser's need to control, this self-blame results in feelings of helplessness rather than empowerment. The feeling of being both responsible for and helpless to stop the violence leads in turn to depression and passivity. This learned depression and passivity makes it difficult for the abused partner to marshal the resources and support system needed to leave." Source

This is how the military conditions you to see the world, except the military no longer physically beats the troops. They can accomplish the same result without leaving a physical mark by yelling, threatening, publicly shaming, imprisoning you, giving you horrible duties and paper work. If all else fails they can send you to remedial military training, which is an unambiguous form of brainwashing used by cults to re-orientate their victim's identity on the in-group.

The end result is that you'll feel guilty for breaking meaningless rules, and you'll attack anyone else you see breaking meaningless rules. And any time anyone criticizes your masters or their agenda you'll defend them to the death oblivious to the fact that you're defending your abuser and attacking anyone who tries to free you from the abuser who has manipulated you into celebrating and defending your own oppression.

3. YOU CAN SUPPORT THE UCMJ OR THE TROOPS BUT NOT BOTH

Many American civilians don't fully understand that military service members fall under a completely separate legal jurisdiction than civilians. This legal code is known as the Uniform Code of Military Justice (UCMJ). The existence of the UCMJ isn't necessarily a sinister thing. In a lot of ways, pointing out that civilians and troops fall under different legal codes is like saying people who work for McDonalds and people who work for Burger King have different employee handbooks. The military is a bureaucratic institution that exists to accomplish a specific purpose just like the United States Post Office. Neither could operate without some kind of guidelines that outline the operating procedures for how they accomplish their purpose.

However, the UCMJ redefines the basic human rights of the people who fall under its jurisdiction in ways that are considered unethical and unconstitutional. It's literally illegal to treat civilians the same way troops are treated under the UCMJ.

You can say you "support the troops" by sending them care packages or putting a yellow ribbon magnet on your car, but that's like a citizen of the Confederate States of America sending care packages to the slaves in the cotton fields and painting "Support the Slaves" on a horse.

Here are 5 ways the UCMJ treats the troops unethically:

1. Bad Conduct and Dishonorable Discharges.

There's effectively no difference between a bad conduct/dishonorable discharge and a felony conviction. No other place of employment has the ability to punish dissenting employees with prison time and felony convictions for not obeying their boss at work. However, the military reserves this right because the UCMJ gives it that right, which is like saying the Bible is true because the Bible says it's true.

Just like how the Bible causes its followers to carry around the burden of the threat of Hell in their minds every time they commit the most innocent, victimless sin, the troops carry around the burden of the threat of a dishonorable discharge with them all the time, everywhere they go. This is tolerable if you don't think about it, but once you realize that the rest of your life will be unceremoniously destroyed if you decide not to do a jumping jack when you're ordered to or you decide not to button up your shirt when you're ordered to and persist in refusing to do so after repeated orders you'll come to realize that your life isn't your own, and your personhood isn't important to the military. You're a slave whose worth is measured by your willingness to conform, and you'll be unceremoniously thrown out onto the street and made an example out of the moment it's convenient for the military.

You can find ways to justify this, but it's a legal fact that McDonald's couldn't do this to its employees because that would be grossly unethical. So let's be clear that in justifying the existence of bad conduct/dishonorable discharges we are in effect justifying second class citizenship for the troops; they have less protection under the law and can be treated worse than other people and we're fine with this.

2. Institutionalized Victimhood/Subjugation.

Imagine if you had to salute teachers, police officers, doctors or politicians any time you pass them in the street. Imagine if you had to address everyone who gets paid more than you as "Sir or

Ma'am." Imagine if you had to deliver these gestures of submission to people you don't work with and don't know. Or imagine if you had to offer these gestures of submission to individuals who you knew for a fact were dumber than you and had less moral character than you.

Now imagine if I told you that you had to salute all these people and address them with a superior title because you respected them....well, that and the fact that if you don't then you'll be demoted, fired, go to jail and/or receive a felony conviction on your permanent employment record that you can't hide from future prospective employers....but the fear of permanent destitution isn't why you salute them. You salute them because you respect them...even if you don't know them or you know for a fact that one of those individuals is a scum bag.

What if I told you that you had to respect these people because they were white, or older than you, or joined the company before you or went to school a little longer than you? In a world where "all men are created equal" does it matter what reason someone tells you to subjugate yourself to another person, especially when the order to subjugate yourself comes with the threat of destitution?

Mandatory gestures of subjugation are reprehensible and illegal in every walk of life except the military, and in that case insult is added to injury by training the troops to glorify participation in their own subjugation. Military training teaches you that the way to be the perfect human is to be the perfect victim or abuser, depending on which side of the caste system your rank places you in relation to the human being standing in front of you.

Again, I understand that there are reasons for the military caste system and for saluting, but those reasons merely justify the exact same level of institutionalized victimhood and subjugation that was imposed on Negro slaves before the Emancipation Proclamation.

Just like with Negro slavery, many honest, well-intentioned people used similar reasons to justify the institutionalized victimhood and subjugation of those slaves, and the worst part is that from one narrow point of view they were right. If you ignore the inherent value of human beings and only look at the well-being of a nation from the standpoint of its economic and political strength, then a caste system looks justifiable. So feel free to argue that the troops need to or deserve to be held to a lower standard of ethical treatment than the civilian population. Just understand that when you do that, saying "Support the Troops" is as meaningful as saying "Support the Niggers."

3. Inhumane Training Methods.

Have you ever wondered why police officers, firemen, lawyers, CEOs or politicians don't go through military basic training? After all, the commercials say that military training will turn you into a super human. If military basic training is such a powerful tool for raising human beings to their full potential then why doesn't everyone or at least the most powerful people in the world go through basic training?

The answer is because military training doesn't raise you to your full potential. It uses time-tested brainwashing techniques to break you down mentally and replace your values and beliefs with those that will ensure you shut down your capacity to reason and question. It indoctrinates you to willfully subjugate yourself to external control and kill without question.

Public and private organizations alike regularly produce literature condemning the training techniques used in military basic training. However, these techniques are only condemned when religious cults use them, not when the military does. I strongly urge you to put this claim to the test. Go look in any brainwashing text book, and compare those methods to military basic training. Military basic training is copied word-for-word from brainwashing textbooks. This isn't a subjective opinion you can disagree with for your own subjective reasons. This is a cut-and-dry, verifiable fact.

Another way you can put this theory to the test is to set up your own basic training camp. Hire ex-basic training instructors to train a group of psychology students using the exact same training manuals and techniques used in military basic training. Then invite the American Psychological Association to monitor your training program for any ethical violations. Your experiment would be shut down before it finished if not before it started.

This raises the question, why the double standards? Why have we taken one group of people and exempted them from the same protections we guarantee everyone else? And does it even matter if there's a reason? What's our freedom worth if it's bought with the blood of slaves and can be taken away from us by our own government with the flick of a pen? Are we even worth protecting if we agree to strip our fellow man of their humanity?

4. Pushing the Limits of Contractual Obligation.

We justify exempting troops from the same rights and protections every other human being is entitled to because the troops signed a contract and took an oath. Actually, this statement is only half true. In the case of a draft the troops don't have a choice. They have to take the oath or go to jail. In that case, the government gets to throw all the rights and protections guaranteed by the constitution out the window at its own discretion. In other words, the government can suspend the constitution at will like it did in the Vietnam War (or as the Vietnamese call it, The American War) when there was zero threat to the American public and the troops were sent in (many against their will) to protect American business's access to the South East Asian economy against the will of the majority of the Vietnamese (and all of the Cambodian) people...but I digress.

The draft sets a precedent that the government can throw out the constitution at will and it doesn't need airtight justification to do so. It can also throw out the constitution if it can get a person to sign a piece of paper waiving their rights. Before you start screaming, "The troops knew what they were getting into before they signed up!" go visit a military recruiter and tell them you want to sign up for the military. They'll put a piece of paper and a pen in front of you and pressure you to sign it as fast as possible.

If you ask them the hard questions about the U.C.M.J. they'll make excuses and dodge the subjects. They'll reassure you everything is on the level and promise you anything they can to get you to sign that paper so they can meet their recruitment quota. They'll even flat out lie to you. Any honest basic training instructor will tell you that military recruiters are synonymous with dishonesty.

To a military apologetisist this is all just nit-picking; the bottom line is the troops signed a contract that's more legally binding than the constitution or the Universal Declaration of Human Rights. I suppose, from a purely technical standpoint that's legally valid. But if that's the case then what the hell are we doing here? If I can just give you a $3,000 kicker bonus and promise to pay for your pregnant wife's upcoming hospital bills (that you can't afford because you work for McDonalds) in exchange for all your civil liberties then why have civil liberties in the first place? The issue here isn't whether or not it's illegal to strip human beings of their civil liberties. The question is whether or not it should be legal. The answer is no. It shouldn't, because as the military says, "A threat to liberty anywhere is a threat to liberty everywhere."

5. Welcome to the Twilight Zone.

Many of the laws in the UCMJ are inoffensive and inarguable. For example, Article 128 of the UCMJ deals with assault. Of course, we don't want people assaulting each other. Article 120 deals with rape. That's a law that I would make a categorical imperative out of. I don't believe that anyone anywhere should be raped for any reason. So I agree with that, but the fact that there are some reasonable lines in the UCMJ doesn't prove that they're all reasonable, practical or just. Look at Articles 133 and 134, which say, "Any commissioned officer, cadet, or midshipman who is convicted of conduct unbecoming an officer and a gentleman shall be punished as a court-martial may direct." and "Though not specifically mentioned in this chapter, all disorders and neglects to the prejudice of good order and discipline in the armed forces, all conduct of a nature to bring discredit upon the armed forces, and crimes and offenses not capital, of which persons subject to this chapter may be guilty, shall be taken cognizance of by a general, special, or summary court-martial, according to the nature and degree of the offense, and shall be punished at the discretion of that court."

If those statements sound borderline meaningless, that's because they are. They were designed as catchall laws to allow the military to incriminate and punish the troops for any reason it subjectively decides. Michelle Manhart was discharged for posing nude in Playboy magazine because it brought discredit on the military. Others have been reprimanded and discharged for moonlighting as strippers even though they kept their daytime job in the military a secret. You'll go to jail and/or get a dishonorable discharge for publicly speaking your mind about morally questionable things your employer (who won't let you quit) is doing. You can be demoted at work for cussing at a minor at a grocery store.

You might not have a problem with this, but let's just be clear about the precedent we're setting here. The military enforces subjective cultural taboos and retains broad discretion in its ability to destroy the lives of its service members for not conforming to the military's narrow perception of morality. Imagine if you were a member of a church, and your pastor found out you cheated on your wife. Then he told your boss and you got demoted at work. Imagine if you got fired at work for marching in a gay pride parade over the weekend. Imagine if you were sentenced to life in prison for whistle-blowing human rights abuses committed by your employer. Would that be fair? Would that be just? No, but that's everyday life for the troops. The human beings are so un-free that they're subject to laws that basically say anything you do can be illegal if your boss wants it to. That's literally the opposite of freedom. That's totalitarian control over the life of a human being, and there's no dignity in that.

Conclusion: All of the extraordinary rules/regulations in the UCMJ are supposedly justified because they ensure good order and discipline, but never forget that this good order and discipline comes at the cost of respect for human dignity and equality. Furthermore, these measures aren't necessary to maintain good order and discipline in the civilian population because civilian employers don't have the same mission as the military. The military's mission is to kill people and blow things up without asking why. This is an unnatural mission that human instincts, common sense and reason-based morality cannot accept. As a result, the military must use invasive techniques to break its members' minds and bind them in an unnatural psychological state against their will if/when necessary. If the military can't break the mind of a troop it will tattoo "failure to conform" on their forehead and throw them in the gutter and make an example of them to scare the remaining troops into submission. To the military, the perfect hero is the perfect slave, and all their benefits and perks are just golden handcuffs. Putting bigger golden handcuffs on the slaves is a hollow way to support them. Refusing to allow open, honest discussion about what the troops are dying/killing for is a hollow way to support them. If you really, truly care about the troops, the best way you can support them is to end the UCMJ and give the troops their rights, their dignity and their freedom back.

4. FOUR REASONS AMERICAN TROOPS ARE AS MUCH VICTIMS AS HEROES

1. Many soldiers are victims of economic oppression.

Many soldiers didn't join the military out of patriotism or the selfless desire to defend other people's freedoms. Many soldiers joined the military for a job; they choose to lock themselves into a nearly unbreakable contract doing an extremely stressful and potentially fatal job because they were poor. They did a cost/benefit analysis of their options in life and came to the conclusion that the risk of dying outweighed the cost of trying to scrape through life in an economic system that shamelessly exploits the poor and limits upward mobility to those who can afford prohibitively expensive college degrees. Any honest military recruiter can corroborate this...though any drill instructor will tell you that there are no honest recruiters.

A military recruiter will likely try to spin this sad fact of life by saying it just proves how great the military is because it saves poor people from a life of destitution, but the only reason the poor are running from a life of destitution is because the political leaders that the military defends are too corrupt and unqualified to create a system where everyone has an equal chance at success.

2. The sole purpose of basic training is brainwashing.

Military personnel have heard that basic training is brainwashing, but they tend to dismiss this accusation as subjective liberal propaganda. It's neither subjective nor propaganda. It's a verifiable fact.

Professor Margaret Singer summed up the definition of brainwashing this way, "Coercive psychological systems are behavioral change programs which use psychological force in a coercive way to cause the learning and adoption of an ideology or designated set of beliefs, ideas, attitudes, or behaviors. The essential strategy used by the operators of these programs is to systematically select, sequence and coordinate many different types of coercive influence, anxiety and stress-producing tactics over continuous periods of time. The techniques fall into seven main categories:

1. Techniques such as: Extended audio, visual, verbal, or tactile fixation drills, excessive exact repetition of routine activities, sleep restriction and/or nutritional restriction.

2. Social isolation is promoted. Contact with family and friends are abridged, as is contact with persons who do not share group-approved attitudes. Economic and other dependence on the group is fostered.

3. Prohibit disconfirming information and non-supporting opinions in group communication. Rules exist about permissible topics to discuss with outsiders. Communication is highly controlled. An "in-group" language is usually constructed.

4. Make the person re-evaluate the most central aspects of his or her experience of self and prior conduct in negative ways. Efforts are designed to destabilize and undermine the subject's basic consciousness, reality awareness, world view, emotional control and defense mechanisms. The subject is guided to reinterpret his or her life's history and adopt a new version of causality.

5. Create a sense of powerlessness by subjecting the person to intense and frequent actions and situations which undermine the person's confidence in himself and his judgment.

6. Create strong aversive emotional arousals in the subject by use of nonphysical punishments such as intense humiliation, loss of privilege, social isolation, social status changes, intense guilt, anxiety and manipulation.

7. Intimidate the person with the force of group-sanctioned secular psychological threats.

These tactics of psychological force are applied to such a severe degree that the individual's capacity to make informed or free choices become inhibited. The victims become unable to make the normal, wise or balanced decisions which they most likely or normally would have made, had they not been unknowingly manipulated by these coordinated technical processes." Source

Every single statement about brainwashing made here is systematically incorporated into military basic training. Military basic training isn't sort of like brainwashing; it's the deliberate perfection of brainwashing, and anyone who is brainwashed is a victim.

3. Soldiers are slaves.

When civilians sign up for the military they sign away most of the civil liberties guaranteed to everyone in the universal declaration of human rights. Many of those soon-to-be-soldiers weren't aware of all the rights they were giving up until after they locked themselves into a legally binding contract. No military recruiter will tell you that you have to read the Uniform Code of Military Justice before enlisting.

Once you do sign your rights away, you literally became the property of and wholly subject to the domination and influence of the U.S. government. That's literally the definition of slavery. That's not speaking metaphorically or bending words in any way. Soldiers are slaves. Period. Slavery is still legal in the "land of the free" because soldiers are slaves, and if living in bondage wasn't unethical enough, the systematic brainwashing soldiers are subjected to manipulates them into loving and celebrating their slave-hood. So soldiers are mental slaves as well as legal slaves.

The fact that the military pays its slaves relatively well and are only subject to slavery for a few years doesn't change the fact that they're still slaves. Even if you disagree with the use of the term "slave," the point remains that they still lose an inhumane, unjust and undignified amount of freedom when they join the military. Granted, some people actually enjoy this way of life, but even if they love and embrace it, that still doesn't change the fact that they're slaves and have lost civil rights that were supposed to be guaranteed to all human beings.

4. Soldiers don't fight for the poor and oppressed. They fight for the rich and powerful.

Many soldiers sleep well at night believing they're liberating the oppressed and protecting civilian's freedoms even if they were once civilians who have now had their freedoms taken away from them and are now being oppressed.

To add to their peace of mind, the U.S. military has been involved in a number of humanitarian missions and will undoubtedly be involved in future humanitarian missions. So from a certain perspective, soldiers are at least inadvertent heroes...or they would be except for the fact that the U.S.

military's primary mission isn't to liberate the oppressed, protect civilian's freedoms or provide humanitarian aid.

Let's assume for the sake of argument that the U.S. military is officially "number one in serving mankind in airlift operations to flood victims, food supply, and rebuilding communities around the world." True as that may be, the U.S. military is currently number one in exporting war, destabilizing regions and killing civilians. A few token presents don't make up for that fact.

It's also arguable how much soldiers serve the American people. Almost half the federal budget goes to the military. Every dollar spent on the military is a tax dollar not spent on education or social services. What do the American people get in return for spending all their taxes on fighting phantom enemies around the globe? They get crumbling schools and pot holes in their roads.

This would be justified if it kept Americans safe and secure at home, but look at Osama Bin Laden. He said himself that the September 11th terrorist attacks were in response to America meddling in Middle Eastern affairs. America's response was to jump into the Middle East with both feet and grow roots. I'm not going to argue whether or not that was the right thing to do, but I will argue that the more bases the American military opens on foreign soil and the more people they kill the more it will piss off the rest of the world and make terrorist attacks more likely.

And since the military is bleeding the American taxpayers out of vital civil services the military is creating ripe conditions for poverty back home, and with poverty comes crime and bloodshed. So even if the U.S. military kills every terrorist in the world it will come home to find a collapsed system where more and more houses have bars on the windows and the police are stretched thin dealing with violent crimes. Every soldier needs to seriously ask themselves if they're really giving or taking more from the American taxpayers.

Conclusion. Look past all the military propaganda about military patriotism, freedom and liberation. Analyze the events leading up to every major military action taken by the United States of America. Analyze the outcome of every major U.S. military action and you'll find very little evidence to back up the claim that the U.S. military's primary mission is to protect freedom or anything else universally idealistic. What you'll find is a consistent theme of war profiteering. Every time America goes to war the rich get richer and the poor get poorer...assuming the poor survive the collateral damage; there are millions who haven't, and there are millions more who won't if business continues as usual. If you're skeptical about this claim (and you should be) then do your research. If you study the facts and not the propaganda you'll find that everything said here is true.

So the question all of this leads up to is: If someone orders you to kill someone else and tells you it's for a very, very, very good reason and you do it with the best of intentions but it turns out that you were lied to and actually killed an innocent person then does that make you a hero, a murderer or a victim? I know it doesn't make you a hero. I don't know if it makes you a murderer, but I do know that it makes you a victim.

5. THE MILITARY IS A CULT

"A cult is a group or movement exhibiting a great or excessive devotion or dedication to some person, idea, or thing and employing unethically manipulative techniques of persuasion and control (e.g., isolation from former friends and family, debilitation, use of special methods to heighten suggestibility and subservience, powerful group pressures, information management, suspension of individuality or critical judgment, promotion of total dependency on the group and fear of leaving it, etc.) designed to advance the goals of the group's leaders to the actual or possible detriment of members, their families, or the community."

I'm going to go through the characteristics of a cult and break down how they apply to military. You'll see by the end of this list that the similarities are too blatant to be explained by accidental coincidence. The more you understand the design of a cult the more obvious it becomes that the military system was painstakingly designed around the cult model.

5 Characteristics of a Destructive Cult

1. "Authoritarian pyramid structure with authority at the top."

There is no system of authority in the world that fits this description more than the military's. All the enlisted grunts with no power are at the bottom, and a few generals who don't get their hands dirty sit at the top raining orders down a clearly defined chain of command that nobody can question. This is an authoritarian pyramid structure.

In military basic training you're forced to sit in classes which teach you the ranks of the pyramid authoritarian structure that you'll have to spend the rest of your enlistment obeying. If you don't follow every single order handed down the authoritarian pyramid structure then you'll go to jail and get a dishonorable discharge.

Military leaders are not leaders. They're dictators. They're dystopian rulers. Military officers are morally equivalent to slave owners. When one human being gets to tell another human being that they have to do whatever they say or else they'll go to jail or be shot then that make the subjugated human being a slave. This is inhumane and violates the basic human rights supposedly guaranteed to all human beings.

The authoritarian pyramid structure of the military is the largest human rights atrocity ever. It's evil. It's unconscionable that anyone would allow this human rights atrocity to exist. Yet it's celebrated by humanity. We should all be ashamed and terrified over how eagerly we celebrate human right atrocities.

2. "Charismatic or messianic leader(s) (Messianic meaning they either say they are God OR that they alone can interpret the scriptures the way God intended."

I used to know an enlisted soldier who had a coffee mug that said, "God couldn't be everyone at once. So he created officers." That coffee mug existed because officers have been compared to gods for years. There was even a movie titled "Gods and Generals." I've often wondered if officers are taught to view themselves as gods in officer training school or if the comparison keeps coming up because they have god-sized egos and god-like power over their subordinates.

Just to remove all doubt of the officer corps claim to surrogate god-hood, all military chaplains are officers. The military has actually coopted religion and injected it into its ranks, and even though the military makes broad attempts to accommodate service members from every faith, if there's ever an irreconcilable conflict of interest between the military's goals and religious doctrine, military law supersedes religious law. Muslims can't pray towards Mecca in the middle of an exercise, and Christians have to kill when ordered to.

Underneath all of this is the ever-pervasive belief that America is God's favored country, and to serve America is to serve God's will. From the Declaration of Independence to every State of the Union address, American politicians align their goals with God's, which means every soldier serves God's will by serving their leaders' will.

3. "Deception in recruitment and/or fundraising."

I really, really hate the common phrase in the military, "You knew what you were getting into when you signed up." In reality, this isn't the case at all (unless you were a military brat). That's why so many people try to commit suicide in basic training. They think the rest of their career is going to be like basic training and they'd rather die. They wouldn't try to commit suicide if they actually knew what they were getting into.

Also, half of basic training is spent in a classroom where you're taught military rules, ranks, and history...because most people don't know anything about it before they're recruited. Part of passing basic training is taking a test to prove you know what you're taught about the military, and very few people make a perfect score on that test. So most people don't even know that much about the military after basic training.

Chances are you don't even know how much you're going to be getting paid before you join. And anyone who has enlisted will tell you their recruiter lied to them about a slew of things. If you don't believe me, go talk to a recruiter. They'll paint you a glorious picture about how the military is a wonderful summer camp that turns you into a man. They'll never mention the indignity you'll suffer and the systematic brainwashing that will strip you of your free will and turn you into a willing slave.

4. "Isolation from society -- not necessarily physical isolation like on some compound in Waco, but this can be psychological isolation -- the rest of the world is not saved, not Christian, not transformed (whatever) -- the only valid source of feedback and information is the group."

This is true on both levels. You're isolated physically in a compound. In basic training during your indoctrination you're totally isolated from the outside world. You're literally locked on base behind barbed wire fences. Later you're shipped all over the world where you don't know anyone and might not even speak the local language.

Ideologically you're separated from the rest of the world by your branch's cult culture. You're told you're better than civilians. You're told you're elite. Your unit has slogans like, "If you ain't Ammo you ain't shit." Or "The best supporting the rest."
You're even told your branch is better than the other branches. You're told you're serving the best government in the world (and thus the rest are inferior). You're told your rank is better than others. You may even have separate dining facilities from the inferior people in your own branch.

Mental and physical isolation are standard practices in the United States military because the military knows how to run an effective cult.

5. "Use of mind control techniques (we use Dr. Robert Jay Lifton's criteria from chapter 22 of his book 'Thought Reform & the Psychology of Totalism' to compare whether the eight psychological and social methods he lists are present in the group at question)."

Military customs and courtesies are designed around the framework of mind control. Let's go through these 8 methods of mind control and see how they all have been systematically incorporated into the military.

1. "Milieu Control: Control of the environment and communication within the environment."

Military bases are completely controlled. They even have laws on them that don't apply to civilian land. Even your clothes are controlled. See what happens if you walk outside without your hat on or leave a button on your shirt unbuttoned. Communication is controlled through the chain of command. And you can't make public statements about the military unless you're a public affairs representative, and even then you have severe restrictions on what you can say.

2. "Mystical Manipulation: Seeks to promote specific patterns of behavior and emotion in such a way that it appears to have arisen spontaneously from within the environment, while it actually has been orchestrated totalist leaders claim to be agents chosen by God, history, or some supernatural force, to carry out the mystical imperative the "principles" (God-centered or otherwise) can be put forcibly and claimed

exclusively, so that the cult and its beliefs become the only true path to salvation (or enlightenment)"

I'll sum this up in one word, "patriotism." What word is more mystical than that? Within the context of patriotism, the best example I can give of "mystical manipulation" is saluting the flag. Twice a day on every military base (that has a loud speaker, which is most of them) the national anthem is played while the American flag is raised or lowered. When this happens, if you're outside, you have to stop whatever you're doing and salute the flag (or salute in the direction the music is coming from if you can't see the flag).

You're told you're doing it out of patriotic respect for the flag. In reality you're doing it because you were told you had to and because you'll be punished if you don't. Would you have ever come up with the idea yourself to stop in the middle of the street on cue to face an inanimate object and put your hand on your head until the music stopped? No. But if you're in the military and you see someone not saluting the flag will you chase down the "perpetrator" and angrily yell at them for their lack of respect and patriotism? Probably. And you'll think it was your idea.

Have you ever asked why soldiers have to keep their boots shined or their uniforms pressed? There's no practical need for it. You might assume that it's because soldiers are well disciplined, but all the soldiers in the military didn't independently come to the same conclusion that it would be responsible to shine their boots and press their uniforms. They were ordered to do that upon fear of severe punishment. The reason soldiers are forced to shine their shoes and press their uniforms is to keep them in the habit of doing whatever their leaders order them to without ever asking why.

3. "Demand for Purity: The world becomes sharply divided into the pure and the impure, the absolutely good (the group/ideology) and the absolutely evil (everything outside the group) one must continually change or conform to the group "norm"; tendencies towards guilt and shame are used as emotional levers for the group's controlling and manipulative influences."

Commander in Chief, George Bush said specifically that the United States military is fighting evil (which makes his side the good or holy side). Capitalism and Communism was divided the same way. We've used the term "axis of evil" more than once. Civilians are even stereotyped by the military as being weak, ignorant and ungrateful.

Within the military organization, the norms of good and evil are constantly being updated, and one must constantly relearn what is right and wrong today. There was a time when blacks, women and homosexuals weren't allowed in the military. Now they're okay. Smoking inside, smoking while walking, and smoking outside designated areas used to be okay. Now they're wrong. Walking while talking on a cell phone used to be okay. Now it's wrong. Every year the uniform changes. I don't know how many times I've seen people break rules like smoking outside a designated area and someone bitched them out and asked, "Where's your integrity?" Integrity has nothing to do with it, but you'll be shamed into conforming to the group norms, and if that doesn't work you'll be punished.

4. "Confession: Cultic confession is carried beyond its ordinary religious, legal and therapeutic expressions to the point of

becoming a cult in itself sessions in which one confesses to one's sin are accompanied by patterns of criticism and self-criticism, generally transpiring within small groups with an active and dynamic thrust toward personal change"

In the military this really only happens in basic training. You're told to admit that before you came into the military you were a useless, undisciplined slob. Now that you're in the military you can wash away your sins by completing basic training and be transformed into a real man. Think of all the Marine commercials you've seen on TV where the guy picks up the sword and is surrounded by light and his clothes change into a crisp, military uniform.

5. "Sacred Science: The totalist milieu maintains an aura of sacredness around its basic doctrine or ideology, holding it as an ultimate moral vision for the ordering of human existence questioning or criticizing those basic assumptions is prohibited a reverence is demanded for the ideology/doctrine, the originators of the ideology/doctrine, the present bearers of the ideology/doctrine offers considerable security to young people because it greatly simplifies the world and answers a contemporary need to combine a sacred set of dogmatic principles with a claim to a science embodying the truth about human behavior and human psychology."

This goes back again to military recruits being told they're fighting for the best nation in the world and that they're in the best branch of their nation's military. Our constitution is even encased in Washington DC in a bullet proof display case, and you're not allowed to take pictures of it. That's not to say the constitution is bad, but it does carry an air of sacredness. Even our money says, "In God we trust." on it. Thus, meaning the preservers of that dollar are protecting something holy. Even the doctrine that takes away the military's human rights is treated as sacred. Recruits are told that the Uniform Code of Military Justice holds them to a "higher" standard than regular people and that they should be proud of it.

6. "Loading the Language: Words are given new meanings -- the outside world does not use the words or phrases in the same way -- it becomes a "group" word or phrase."

There are pamphlets and even classes for new spouses of military members that teach them the new language of the military so they'll know what it means when their spouse says, "Before I go to the BX to pick up my BDUS. I'm taking the POV to the MPF to pick up my PCS orders to my next OCONUS assignment, which should be somewhere in USAFE."

7. "Doctrine Over Person: If one questions the beliefs of the group or the leaders of the group, one is made to feel that there is something inherently wrong with them to even question -- it is always "turned around" on them and the questioner/criticizer is questioned rather than the questions answered directly the underlying assumption is that doctrine/ideology is ultimately more valid, true and real than any aspect of actual human character or human experience and one must subject one's experience to that "truth" the experience of contradiction can be immediately associated with guilt one is made to feel that doubts are reflections of one's own evil when doubt arises, conflicts become intense."

I have personal experience with this. One of my supervisors asked me point blank why I wanted to get out of the military (after I already received my approval for separation). So I told him my reasons. A week later I was forced to re-swear my oath of allegiance to the military and the constitution.

You won't last in the military if you just view it as a day job. You're expected to buy into all the ideology. You're expected to associate your identity with the military and be proud of it. Anything less and you'll be ostracized by the group and bullied at work.

8. "Dispensing of Existence: Since the group has an absolute or totalist vision of truth, those who are not in the group are bound up in evil, are not enlightened, are not saved, and do not have the right to exist; impediments to legitimate being must be pushed away or destroyed one outside the group may always receive their right of existence by joining the group; fear manipulation -- if one leaves this group, one leaves God or loses their salvation/transformation, or something bad will happen to them; the group is the "elite", outsiders are "of the world", "evil", "unenlightened", etc."

I've already covered this enough that I don't feel the need to retype it. If you need more validation then go ask a Marine how they feel about POGs and civilians.

SOURCE:
http://www.csj.org/studyindex/studycult/study_whatisdescult.htm

6. HOW AND WHY BASIC TRAINING BRAINWASHES RECRUITS

The premise of my argument is that the United States military's rules, customs, "courtesies," and overall culture did not evolve organically. They were consciously and systematically designed using modern psychological research on mind control and are based on professional knowledge of how cults indoctrinate and control their followers' minds. I can't prove this argument by sourcing internal documents or training manuals, but if you compare how the United States military operates to how cults operate you'll see that the similarities aren't vague or coincidental; the United States military is the perfection of the cult model. If you want to start a cult you'll have the best chance of success by copying the United States military's rules, customs, courtesies and overall culture as closely as possible.

It all starts with the recruiting process. All cults use deceptive recruiting methods. When they approach you on the street or draw you into their recruiting stations they promise you everything glorious in life and death you could ever want while dodging and skimming over the negative aspects of what your life will be like in their organization. They never explain in detail all the rules you'll be subjected to or how they'll manipulate you into basing your identity on your role in their organization. The United States military is no different. If you go into any recruiter station they'll promise you money, benefits, travel and glory, but they'll never mention the U.C.M.J, and if you point out any negative aspects of the military they'll make any excuse they can think of to dismiss your concern or glaze over it.

You'll never get a military recruiter to admit that the United States military is a cult, because they probably don't realize it is. Cults don't advertise themselves as cults. They don't tell their recruits they're joining a cult. They indoctrinate their recruits to believe that they're joining the noblest organization in the world. Then they send their brainwashed followers out to recruit more recruits. So even if all the original, malicious leaders at the top of the cult's pyramid shaped authority structure die and there's no one left alive who knows that the organization was systematically designed around manipulation techniques, the cult will still continue to function. Its brainwashed followers will run on autopilot brainwashing new recruits like a virus. There may still be leaders at the top level of the United States military who understand that their rules, customs, courtesies and overall culture are precisely cultish, but there doesn't need to be. It is a cult, and it will continue to operate on autopilot in the absence of willful manipulation.

As a result military recruiters willingly volunteer to act like used car salesmen and wrangle poor people into joining by promising them that all their dreams will come true if they just sign a legally binding contract (something every other cult must wish they could do). What those recruiters won't tell you is that they have a quota that they have to meet, and they get rewards for exceeding it, which is another reason the cult is able to continue to run on auto pilot. Its recruiters must bring in new recruits whether they want to or not, because if they don't they'll get in trouble, but if they do they'll be rewarded with treasures of this world regardless of whether or not they're true believers.

Once the military convinces the recruit to sign all their civil liberties away the recruit is taken to a hotel where they'll be watched and kept from running away the day before they begin their indoctrination process. The recruits will be told that on the next day they'll be taken to a training facility where they'll learn how to be an adult and an efficient worker. But in reality, they won't learn anything about being an adult, and they'll learn very little about their job, because that's not the point of basic training. The point of basic training is to break down the recruits' sense of identity and indoctrinate them to base their identity on their membership within the cult.

If the United States military has done its job right then any prior service or active duty military member reading this will be screaming, "That's not what basic training is about! It prepares you to follow orders because when the shit hits the fan on the battle field you have to act without thinking in order to keep yourself and your fellow soldiers alive!"

That's what the military tells its recruits to believe, and that argument sounds good on paper, but if you scratch the surface you'll find flaws in that argument. Firstly, the majority of the humans who go through the military's indoctrination process will never see the battle field. Millions of them will never even leave the continental United States. But they go through the same indoctrination process because the purpose of basic training isn't to prepare you for the battlefield. Its purpose is to ensure that every recruit will always blindly serve the interests of their leaders, and the leadership hierarchy stacks up like this: Enlisted troops take orders from officers. Officers take orders from politicians, and politicians take orders from the individuals and special interest groups who fund their campaigns, give them bribes and employ them after they leave public service. Thus, military members are unwitting mercenaries for (and blind supporters of) the ultra-rich. The United States military serves the interests of the wealthy. Every major military campaign the United States military has been involved in has made the rich richer and the poor poorer. And the gears of war and profit will keep turning as long as nobody in the military ever dissents or asks questions. That's why it's imperative that every recruit be systematically brainwashed to associate their identity primarily with their membership in the military.

The process of reprogramming civilians begins the second they step off the bus and set foot on their basic training base. The moment they leave the bus they're descended upon by multiple drill sergeants or training instructors. Different branches call their basic instructors by different names. Each branch also has different names for their ranks, career fields and facilities. The reason for this is because it causes members of each branch to base their identity on their respective branch. This makes it less likely for military personnel to form a coup against their corrupt political leaders.

Differentiating the branches from each other serves another purpose as well. It's standard procedure for cults to indoctrinate their members to believe that anyone who isn't a member of the cult is inferior. Every military member is taught that civilians are untried, unproven and take their livelihood for granted while the glorious military sacrifices everything and is better than everyone else (regardless of the fact that many military members will spend their career sitting at a desk stateside for 20 years living rent-free, receiving free medical care and driving a Ford Mustang that they paid for with their reenlistment bonus). Pitting military members against civilians is a powerful mind control technique that the military reuses by pitting military members against each other.

Airmen (aka "Zoomies") are taught they're smarter than Marines (aka "Jar Heads"). Marines are taught they're tougher than soldiers (aka "Grunts"). Special Forces are taught they're better than regular infantry. All combatants are taught they're better than POGs, and everyone thinks the Navy is gay. Pitting each branch against each other doesn't cause them to go to war with each other though. It causes each branch to be even more loyal to its own chain of command, and since the entire military falls under the command of the Department of Defense, whoever controls the D.O.D benefits from this manufactured infighting.

But I digress. When recruits get off the bus their first day of basic training they're immediately set upon by a flock of "training instructors" who throw hell at them. The instructors yell at them, insult them, tear them down, threaten them and tell them they don't deserve to be there. The purpose of this initial assault is to shock and awe the new recruits. It makes them doubt themselves as well as accept the authority of anyone wearing the cult's symbols of rank on their shoulders. All of this primes them to be receptive to the message they'll be inundated with over the next few weeks.

Every year billions of people around the world enter employment in jobs that are just as dangerous if not more dangerous than what the average American military recruit signs up for, but they aren't subjected to the mental abuse American troops are subjected to on their first day, yet they still follow orders and go above and beyond the call of duty often putting themselves at unnecessary personal risk. You don't need to assault a human's mind to convince them to do what's necessary. But you do need to assault their mind if you want to reprogram their identity.

The next form of mental assault that the American government submits its military recruits to is less obvious but just as important to the indoctrination process. The recruits are filed into dormitories or barracks where they'll live in communal spaces with up to 60 other people. They'll have absolutely no privacy or control over their environment. Everything they own will be identical to everyone else there. Everyone will dress the same and looks the same. Everyone will sleep in identical beds and keep what few possessions they're allowed to have in identical lockers. They'll even have to shower naked in communal showers with dozens of other recruits. All of these factors dehumanize the new recruits and help break down their sense of identity and self-worth.

The lack of privacy breaks down the recruit's defenses. You can't hold up your guard when you're naked in a shower with 15 other people and sleeping in a room with 30 other people. Under those circumstances you're like a vulnerable child who has no home, no identity, no safe haven, no escape, no choices and no power over your own destiny. You're nobody. And the only source of validation you can possibly experience comes from the cult, which makes the cult your mother, your father, your boss and your god.

If this doesn't seem sinister yet, consider that the new recruits will be held captive within the confines of their dormitory. A sentinel will stand guard at the entrance preventing anyone from leaving, and if an escapee can manage to get out of the building they'll still be trapped on base behind tall fences lined with razor wire as well as gate guards armed with semi-automatic assault rifles. The military holds a gun to its recruits' heads and forces them to endure the indoctrination process, which is so mentally brutal that many recruits will attempt suicide.

The military goes through such dire lengths to keep its recruits locked away from the outside world because it's much harder to break down and reprogram someone's identity when they don't have access to their old support structures or the freedom to live life by their own accord. So you have to isolate them from everything they've ever known and inundate them completely with the rules, customs and culture of cult. When the cult is all they know... then the cult is all they know. Once the recruits spend a few weeks eating, sleeping and breathing nothing but the cult's way of life they'll accept that that's how life is. And why wouldn't they? The reality of their day to day life is whatever the cult makes it. So they go about their day to day life experiencing reality according to how the cult defines it, and in no time at all, they take the cult's way of life for granted.

Isolating new recruits from the outside world also insulates them from dissent and freedom of thought. If the recruits go out on the town every night or even worse, go home, they might tell someone about all the new things they've been learning. Then someone with a free mind might point out how crazy they sound and convince them to leave the cult.

Another reason cult members are forced to live in communal quarters is because humans take cues from other people's behavior and mimic it. You'd have a very hard time taking a lone individual to an empty camp and convincing them to change their behavior. However, if you take 60 people and force them to all behave the same way they'll assume that since everyone else is going along with it then it must be okay. Plus, once you break the minds of the weakest members they'll take it upon themselves to enforce the rules of the group.

With the stage set the instructors can begin actively reprogramming the minds of their recruits. The daily indoctrination process begins as soon as the recruits wake up each morning. Loudspeakers in the ceilings of the dormitories blast a trumpet tune called reveille often times accompanied by training instructors banging trash can lids and shouting at the recruits telling them to get up and quit being lazy. The recruits will have a few minutes to get dressed, make up their bed and line up in formation outside.

The brain-rattling trumpet, combined with the frantic morning chores and the instructor's insults throws the recruits off center from the moment they wake ensuring that they won't have the mental focus to resist the indoctrination process. The chores and routines also ensures that the recruits are following orders from the moment they wake up even if the instructor isn't even present to tell them to get dressed, make up their beds and file outside for formation. Thus the military controls every aspect of their lives and leaves no room for individual freedom of thought or action. The more the recruits accept that as the norm the less likely they are to question it and the more likely they are to embrace it.

There are very specific rules for falling into formation. Following those rules first thing in the morning continues to reinforce blind obedience to the group without questioning the purpose of orders. Standing in the group formation where everyone looks and acts identically also helps minimize the individuality of the group members. In case the recruits don't pick up on this idea on their own the training instructors will tell them bluntly that they're no longer an individual. They're a member of the group, and their own identity and desires are worth less than the identity and desires of the group. Training instructors will tell the recruits to be proud of this fact and to look down on civilians who value their individuality and selfishly desire to fulfill their own destiny.

Any active duty or prior service members reading this will likely be screaming, "But you should value being a member of the group! That creates a stronger team and keeps the group together when the shit hits the fan! Anyway, we're proud to put our own egos aside to help protect the freedom of civilians!"

Those criticisms aren't wrong, but there's more going on than just that. First, there's the fact that the military isn't upfront about the invasive methods of mind control it submits its troops to, and that's unethical. Also, reprogramming recruits sense of identity eliminates their freedom to determine their own destiny. It makes mental slaves out of recruits who are so zealous that they'll defend their own manipulation. This reprogramming controls all aspects of the brainwashed victim's life, not just how they perform their job. Plus, reprogramming individuals essentially kills the person they once were and creates a new person. Once the old person is dead they can never come back to life as the person they once were. Doing that to another human being is no small matter, and no human has the authority and right to kidnap another person's soul. Finally, it's worth noting that everyone in the world will participate as a functional member of a team on an almost daily basis without being brainwashed. Sports teams are high functioning teams that coordinate plays selflessly without going through a brutal indoctrination process. Even civilian contractors in the military play by the rules and make sacrifices in war zones without going through basic training.

Once the recruits are lined up in their morning formation they sing their branch's official song and chant an oath of allegiance to the military and the United States. This is cut and dry, unambiguous brainwashing 101.

After having sworn their daily oath of allegiance the troops eat breakfast, and even then they don't get a moment to themselves. They have to file through the cafeteria silently standing heel to toe, staring straight ahead while instructors hover over them to punish anyone who breaks these arbitrary rules. When the recruits finally get their food they'll be given as little time as possible to eat to ensure they can't relax and mentally collect themselves.

After the meal they'll take part in physical exercises and marching drills. They'll perform their exercises and marching drills as a group, everyone acting in unison further conditioning them to base their identity on the group. Every member of the group will be punished whenever any individual fails to follow the arbitrary rules perfectly. This encourages the recruits to police each other. The more the recruits enforce the military's rules on each other the more they take the military's rules and authority for granted.

The military doesn't leave this powerful mind control technique to chance. The instructors will assign recruits as element leaders. The element leaders will receive an arbitrary symbol of authority (a colored rope that attaches to the lapel of their uniform), and they'll be tasked with policing their group. When the military leadership bestows authority on individuals it teaches every member of the group that the military has the authority to bestow authority on individuals and raise their value as a human being. Once the recruits take this for granted they'll always respect higher ranking military members as if God Himself touched their leaders with His grace. Finally, it dangles a carrot in front of the recruits. They're taught in basic training that their life is worthless outside of the military hierarchy and that elevation within the cult is the true path to elevation as a person. The use of "ropes" or element leaders sets this precedent from day one.

This is also why recruits are called "trainees" instead of Airmen, soldiers, seamen or Marines. They have to prove themselves worthy first before being granted a title in the illustrious group. Every cult in the world does this. The military just hides this brainwashing technique in plain sight.

At some point during the day, between eating, exercising and marching the recruits will be taken to classrooms where they'll receive hundreds of hours of lectures on military history, rules and customs. The point of teaching military history is to train the recruits to accept the military's history as their own history. Once they come to base their identity on hundreds of years of history they've just learned they'll always view themselves as a member of that distinct group.

If any troop ever complains about life in the military they'll be told, "You knew what you were getting into before you signed up." But the hundreds of hours of class time they'll spend in basic training betray this lie. You won't learn all the details of what you signed up for until you take these classes.

Those classes teach all the unique symbols, language, rules, customs and beliefs that make up the overall military culture. On the surface most of them are innocuous, but it's standard operating procedure for cults to manufacture their own internal culture based on shared symbols, terminology, rules and customs, because you need to give the recruits a culture to latch onto and derive their new identity from. The whole point of giving recruits a new culture and a new identity is to tie it all into the group's pyramid shaped leadership hierarchy. All the other details are red herrings, but once you accept them you'll accept your place in the leadership hierarchy that comes along with it. From then on you'll always respect and obey any human being who wears the arbitrary symbols that represent authority within the cult.

After class (and maybe a few more marching drills) the recruits are filed back into their dormitories where they'll spend the rest of their night cleaning their rooms, organizing their lockers, folding their clothes and arranging their belongings to precise requirements. The purpose of these chores is to simply get the recruits used to obeying arbitrary rules. If you can get them to perform mundane tasks without question you can get them to perform any task without question.

It also gives the instructors more reasons to berate the recruits and tear down their sense of self-worth (and just as importantly) to reward the recruits for demonstrating obedience. In a stressful, totalitarian environment a simple bar of candy or a phone call home is worth a million dollars. Recruits will love their captors when given these small token rewards.

Throughout the whole indoctrination process the instructors will find any reason in the world to make the recruits doubt their worth as a person and as a member of the group. As they tear down the recruits they'll slowly build them back up with praise and rewards. Then, just as the recruits are beginning to feel good about themselves the instructor will find any excuse to tear them back down again. If the recruits are doing everything right the instructor will simply lie and tell them they're all failing at their duties. This emotional roller coaster keeps the recruits doubting their worth, makes them yearn to win the approval of their captors and makes them feel more proud when they receive any sign of affection or validation. It's a way to systematically induce Stockholm Syndrome.

By the end of basic training the effects of the reprogramming techniques will have taken root in the trainee's minds. They'll sing their branch song with pride, gush when they see an officer and perform every task asked of them with gusto. In the end they'll take part in a lavish ceremony where they'll receive the mark of the in-group and will be congratulated on their elevation to true worth as a member of the group cementing the effects of the indoctrination process.

After reading all this you may still hold firm that military basic training teaches discipline and trains recruits to act without hesitation as a member of a goal-oriented team. As true as that may be, and as useful as that may be, it's still not the whole truth. The fact of the matter remains that the training methods used in basic training are the exact same methods used by cults, and they have the exact same results. They rob recruits of their identity and replace it with a willing mental slave drunk on loyalty to the in-group. The training methods used on military recruits are considered unethical and even illegal to do anyone else, and they're so invasive and brutal that they cause the recruits extreme mental anguish in the process to the point that many even attempt to commit suicide.

I have never seen evidence to support the claim that is absolutely necessary to submit human beings to this form of unethical treatment in order to create a smoothly functioning organization. Even if it were, we still have to ask ourselves if the cost is worth it, especially since it contradicts the entire reason the military supposedly exists: to protect the freedom and dignity of the citizens of the United States.

7. THE PARALLELS BETWEEN THE STANFORD PRISON EXPERIMENT AND TECH SCHOOL

"The Stanford prison experiment was a study of the psychological effects of becoming a prisoner or prison guard. The experiment was conducted from August 14th to 20th, 1971 by a team of researchers led by psychology professor Philip Zimbardo at Stanford University. It was funded by a grant from the U.S. Office of Naval Research and was of interest to both the US Navy and Marine Corps in order to determine the causes of conflict between military guards and prisoners.

Twenty-four students were selected out of 75 to play the prisoners and live in a mock prison in the basement of the Stanford psychology building. Roles were assigned randomly. The participants adapted to their roles well beyond what even Zimbardo himself expected, leading the "Officers" to display authoritarian measures and ultimately to subject some of the prisoners to torture. In turn, many of the prisoners developed passive attitudes and accepted physical abuse, and, at the request of the guards, readily inflicted punishment on other prisoners who attempted to stop it. The experiment even affected Zimbardo himself, who, in his capacity as "Prison Superintendent," lost sight of his role as psychologist and permitted the abuse to continue as though it were a real prison. Five of the prisoners were upset enough by the process to quit the experiment early, and the entire experiment was abruptly stopped after only six days. The experimental process and the results remain controversial. The entire experiment was filmed, with excerpts made publicly available."

The Stanford Prison Experiment was shut down because it violated the ethical standards of professional psychology resulting in psychological and physical harm to the subjects in the experiment. However, the exact same scenario has been repeated every day since before the 1970s on every military tech school in America with full immunity from the law and a deliberate disregard for the ethical treatment of humans.

Here's how tech school works. Once a soldier (aka airman, marine or seaman) graduates basic training they're sent to a "tech school" to learn the job skill they'll perform for the rest of their career in the military. While life in tech school isn't as rigorous as basic training, it is the last chance for the military to conform its troops' thoughts and behavior to its standards before releasing them into "the real military" to succeed or fail at supporting real world missions. So the environment is designed to indoctrinate the students to embrace willful obedience and let go of their pre-military identity. Troops live in barracks and are granted small freedoms (such as the right to wear civilian clothing and leave the base) in stages to decompress them from the totalitarian internment they experienced in basic training. In tech school, the troops march to and from school in uniform and are assigned some additional duties after school. Many aspects of life for the students are highly regulated in ways that serve no functional purpose other than to get them used to following rules without question. You can't walk on the grass. You have to carry a flashlight at night. Your uniform must be immaculate. Your room must be cleaner than Martha Stewart's dream home, etc.

So far the standard operating procedure of military tech school exactly mirrors (because it's based on) the standard operating procedures of a cult, which is unethical in itself and would be shut down by the government if any other organization other than the government attempted to use similar methods.

The parallels between the Stanford Prison Experiment are found in the use of student leaders or "ropes." The student leaders are responsible for policing their fellow students. On paper, these duties can be made to sound innocuous and clinical to the point of boredom. In reality what happens is the student leaders have a tendency to mimic the intensity and righteous fury of the training instructors and drill sergeant they've been getting yelled at by for the past 6-9 weeks. The student leaders tend to feel and express genuine disappointment and anger over the smallest infraction regardless of how arbitrary the rule being violated is. They'll scream at their subordinates for walking on the grass and accuse them in all seriousness (with no sense of irony) for having no integrity.

This behavior isn't an anomaly, and it doesn't happen behind the backs of the senior military leader's running the school. It's actively encouraged and built into the tech school's official operating procedures. In order for a student leader to advance to the highest level of student leadership, they must "host" "remedial military training." When a student has violated enough arbitrary rules they're assigned a day of remedial military training over the weekend. During that time they'll be forced to exercise beyond the point of exhaustion and submit themselves to a full day of verbal degradation. Remedial military training is overseen by senior ranking sergeants, but the details are run by the student leaders.

The military justifies this behavior by saying it's necessary to instill discipline, but that's just an Orwellian way to say, "brainwashing." To be fair, it's not like they're taping troops' eyes open, feeding them gunpowder and forcing them to watch snuff films. Having said that, the end result of the brainwashing techniques used in tech school is that the followers of the military cult will someday kill another human being without question.

At any rate, the point is that the "training" methods used by the military are literally in direct violation of professional standards of the ethical treatment of human beings. This exact same behavior has already been shut down by the government in the Stanford Prison Experiment. This isn't an opinion. This isn't said out of spite or ridicule. This is a cut and dried fact. If a professional civilian psychologist recreated the exact same environment that exists in military tech schools, much less basic training, their simulation would be shut down by the government for ethics violations. Period.

This raises a very serious point that deserves to be considered seriously and objectively. Soldiers, airmen, seaman and marines are human beings. However, the government, which is run by human beings, has written the Uniform Code of Military Justice to provide a loophole around the Universal Declaration of Human Rights and exempt military personnel from the same ethical protection guaranteed to everyone else. The only justification for this I have ever heard is that it is necessary to protect our rights and freedoms. That argument is self-defeating. It says we have to strip the rights of one portion of society, legalize their systematic emotional, psychological and physical abuse and literally enslave them in order to prevent the rest of society from suffering the exact same fate. Then, to add insult to injury, we're then told to "support the troops."

I don't support the unethical treatment of the human beings we've labeled "troops." I don't support the fact that they've lost their freedom. I don't support the military caste system. I don't support slaves being led to get slaughtered in wars their leaders can't give proper justifications for. I don't support the UCMJ that allows all of this to happen.

I do support ending the UCMJ. I support freeing the human beings we call troops. I support equal rights for all people, even those who have been coerced and misled into signing away their rights "voluntarily." And I don't believe the only way we can achieve peace and harmony on earth is to enslave one portion of society, strip them of their identity and reprogram them into unthinking killers. I believe the standard operating procedures of the United States military are in direct conflict with creating a peaceful and harmonious world. I believe that if you truly "support the troops" then you cannot support the UCMJ that allows the unethical treatment of your fellow human beings, especially those you claim to support and call heroes.

8. AN OVERDUE CRITIQUE OF THE MILITARY CASTE SYSTEM

The American military caste system, particularly its officer corps, is an obsolete institution that is incompatible with modern, enlightened values. In order to understand why this is you have to look at where it came from. In the past, the upper class was extremely well educated, and the poor were mostly illiterate. The job of designing and implementing military strategy naturally fell to the educated upper class, and the job of dying in the mud naturally fell to the illiterate lower class. This division of labor also served as a way to further institutionalize the caste system that separated the upper class from the lower class. By putting a pin on one human being's shoulder and a stripe on another human being's shoulder it gave one human being a visible "right" to order the other like a dog, beat them like a dog and kill them like a dog if they disobeyed their master's orders. As long as these symbols existed everyone understood their place in the social hierarchy and accepted it as natural and just.

The industrial revolution and the information age eventually created a middle class to bridge the income gap between the rich and the poor. The higher education system still keeps a glass ceiling over the heads of the poorest of the poor who can't afford a college degree to open the door to professional work. However, free K-12 public schools, equal access to libraries and all the information on the internet has almost completely bridged the intellectual gap between the rich and the poor.

The constitution of the United States, the Bill of Rights and the Universal Declaration of the Human Rights (to name just a few relevant legal documents) have whittled the institutionalized caste system down to a thread. These new social contracts have even affected the United States military. Senior ranking soldiers can no longer legally beat lower ranking soldiers. All soldiers are guaranteed protection from discrimination based on race, sex or religion under equal opportunity laws. Technically, a soldier can still be executed for disobeying a direct order, but that involves a lengthy legal process, and in order to avoid the bad press, disobedient soldiers are almost guaranteed to just do some jail time followed by a dishonorable discharge.

But the military has side-stepped social progress by inventing the Uniform Code of Military Justice (UCMJ). This document exists to provide the military with a legal loophole around the basic human rights guaranteed to all of humanity. One of the greatest insults to humanity perpetrated by the UCMJ is the existence of the officer corps.

The injustice of the officer corps is most clearly exemplified in the act of saluting. When an enlisted troop sees an officer (or a general's staff car) they must put their hand on their head until the officer returns the salute, which gives the enlisted troop permission to take their hand down. On the surface this is innocuous. Officers will even tell you that the reason enlisted troops salute them is out of respect. However, the true purpose of saluting is betrayed by what will happen if an enlisted troop refuses to salute an officer.

If an enlisted troop refuses to salute an officer they'll get a letter of counseling. If they still refuse to salute an officer they'll get a letter of reprimand. Then an Article 15. Then a court martial. Then they'll lose rank, pay, privilege and ultimately their freedom when they're sent to jail. When they're released from military prison they'll be given a dishonorable discharge that will prevent them from getting a good job for the rest of their life.

Enlisted troops are taught to salute officers out of respect, but failing that, they're forced to salute officers out of fear. While the rest of the population is guaranteed that their punishment must fit their crime, enlisted troops and lower ranking officers are denied this right and are forced to symbolically subjugate themselves to any stranger wearing a pin on their shoulder. So make no mistake, the salute isn't designed to exchange gestures of respect. It's designed to systematically indoctrinate lower ranking troops to accept their place in the lower social caste that robs them of the dignity supposedly guaranteed to all men.

And the issue goes deeper than dignity. An officer can order enlisted troops to do anything within the limits of the Geneva Convention, and if the enlisted troop refuses they'll go to jail. For example, if the higher caste orders the lower caste to do jumping jacks and the lower cast refuses they'll go to jail. On the surface, this might seem innocuous again, but look at what's really going on here. What do you call someone who has to do whatever another person says upon fear of jail time and destitution? That's a slave, and even if you think "slave" is too strong a word to describe someone with no freedom, it's still close enough to the truth to be immoral and unenlightened.

If you're going to justify the manipulation, exploitation, degradation and subjugation of another human being, much less an entire group of human beings, you have the responsibility to provide extensive, articulate, air-tight justifications. You can't wipe away thousands of years of social evolution and human rights with a vague sentence or two such as, "Well, they took an oath." "They volunteered." "Good soldiers follow orders." "You're an idiot." or "You have to follow orders to accomplish the mission."

This is especially true when we're talking about soldiers who will be ordered to kill other human beings and be killed themselves in the process. This isn't a game. This isn't a joke. This is a human's life we're putting on trial, and in the case of a military with nuclear weapons, this is the fate of the entire human race we're talking about. When we're talking about tangible, perishable human lives, we can't afford to be lackadaisical in our arguments. If you truly believe that the lower military castes are selflessly sacrificing their lives for the greater good then they, of all people, deserve serious consideration and not just flippant, condescending, reactionary excuses and arguments about semantics.

Honestly ask yourself if the officer corps and the human rights abuses that come along with it are truly necessary. In the past, the officer corps' power and their pay were justified by the degree to which their education level and thus their contribution to the mission exceeded that of the enlisted troop. This arrangement held some merit when the average officer held the equivalent of a doctorate degree and the average enlisted troop held the equivalent of a 3rd-grade education, but that justification is obsolete.

Many enlisted troops have a higher level of education than many officers even if they don't have the certified credentials to prove it, though some do. Even in the cases where officers do have a higher level of education, that fact doesn't supersede the fact that all humans were created equal. An officer may have gone to 1-4 more years of school and a few months of officer training school, but to presume that that gives one human being the inherent right to treat another human being as anything remotely resembling a slave and force them to degrade themselves is absurd.

Civilian doctors can't treat uneducated patients like that. Public school teachers can't treat students like that. Politicians can't treat voters like that. Prison guards can't even treat rapists like that. Nobody in the world is allowed to treat anyone else with the level of disrespect that officers are allowed and expected to treat enlisted troops with.

After all, why should they be able to? Do a few years of partying in college really fundamentally change the worth of a human being? If so, shouldn't all of society adopt this practice? If this system is indeed justifiable then shouldn't we force it on the rest of society? No! It would be inconceivable to force 100% of society to live under an institutionalized caste system that degrades the lower class. It would inconceivable to force even 50% or 30% of the population to live that way. So why is it okay for 1% of the population to live under a dystopian social contract?

What would happen if troops were as free as civilians? What if they could give a two-week notice and quit their job legally? What if they could challenge and disobey their "superiors?" The existing power structure would have you believe the entire military would dissolve into anarchy. Is that really logical though? The United States has an all-volunteer military. Why would people who willingly volunteered to join the military and support its mission turn around at their first base and abandon their jobs? If you think they would then you're saying all the troops are cowards. Even civilians who work for the military don't turn tail and run at the first sign of danger.

The only other exception is if the mission were unjust. If there were a valid reason to conscientiously object to the mission then any troop with foresight and a sense of justice would leave their military service. This raises the question, what are the chances the government would ever engage in an unjust war or send its troops on unjust missions? If you're 100% positive the government would never, ever do that, then why lock the troops into anything remotely resembling slavery? If you believe the government has ever engaged in unjust wars, ordered its troops to do unjust things or will ever do so then you would want the troops to have the freedom to think and act on their own conscience. Preventing them from doing so by brainwashing them and holding a gun to their heads would only guarantee corrupt and/or misguided politicians the ability to call on the world's most lethal fighting force to serve their corrupted purposes. When you justify the enslavement of the military, you need to understand lucidly that you're giving a monkey a gun on blind faith.

And understand the irony of saying, "Yes, we must brainwash troops, lock them into a caste system and take away their freedom." What you're saying is that we absolutely must mislead, mentally and physically enslave and degrade our fellow human beings into submission...for the sake of protecting our fellow human beings from slavery, abuse and exploitation. The United States Military failed its mission of protecting people's freedoms the moment it threw out the Universal Declaration of Human Rights out the window in favor of the Uniform Code of Military Justice.

Honestly, what are we doing here? What kind of a world are we creating where we've justified an oppressive caste system at the taxpayers' expense to act as unquestioning mercenaries for the rich and powerful? How can we honestly say to ourselves that we "support the troops" when we've allowed our brothers and sisters to be swindled out of their basic human rights?

Are we even worth defending when we would so proudly throw our fellow man under the bus like that? What kind of a world are we creating? You can see with your own eyes what kind of a world we're creating. Go to any American military base in the world and tour the officer's barracks and clubs. Then tour the enlisted barracks and clubs. You should be horrified by the Soviet-era disparity between the quality of life between the two castes. The officers gorge themselves on luxury in gold-encrusted rooms (paid for by impoverished taxpayers) while the enlisted people shiver in condemned buildings. You'll see a world that has existed right under your nose for your entire life that makes "1984" look like a children's story.

Don't accept the American military's actions on blind faith alone. If the military's actions have truly been just, then go to the all the countries America has exported war to this century. Talk to the people and look at the physical results of the war. Oh, you'll find people who celebrate the American military, but for every one of those you find you'll find 1000 corpses, 1000 broken families, 1000 babies with birth defects from discarded military ordinance, 1000 destroyed buildings, 10 sweat shops where American goods are produced and more often than not, a few active American military bases.

Suppose everything I've said here is wrong. Suppose the military caste system is excusable despite its indignity. We (or at least the taxpayers who maintain it) still need to question its efficiency. We've already asked ourselves if we should have absolute faith in the politicians who wield unquestionable control over the military and acknowledged the inherent danger in that. Now consider this. Think of all the civilians you know with a bachelor's degree. What if they had absolute, unquestionable authority over the subordinates in their cubicles. How responsibly would they wield their power to silence all opposition to their will by saying, "Shut up and color or I'll send you to jail."? Would totalitarian authority improve innovation and efficiency in public or private organizations? Is there any precedent whatsoever to suggest that totalitarian authority has a tendency to inculcate close-minded thinking, abuse of power and impunity from accountability? Yes. Civilian progress would grind to a halt if they adopted the same caste system the United States military uses. The military is made up of human beings, just like the civilian sector, and the caste system has had predictably detrimental effects in the military. The military sets the standard for fraud, waste and abuse because it's run by the officer corps, which is fraud, waste and abuse incarnate.

There's one final cost to the officer corps itself that we have to acknowledge and accept if we're to continue to condone its existence much less its celebrity status. Look at the psychological damage it does to officers when they're allowed to exercise totalitarian authority over other human beings they call their subordinates. Consider the psychological impact it has on a human being when they're treated like a god day in and day out for years. This lifestyle will take its toll. The constant reinforcement will indoctrinate the officer himself to truly believe there is something superior about his person, and when this belief is indoctrinated deeply enough he'll eventually reach a point where this illusion becomes permanent reality in their own mind. Then they'll go through the rest of their life wearing rose-colored glasses. They'll live in an inescapable false reality in which they play a divine figure walking amongst unclean, incomplete sub-humans, and while this will be enjoyable to the officer, it's simply not true. That's literally insanity. The officer corps is institutionalized insanity. I don't say that to shame officers, I say that to shame the taxpayers who fund the indoctrination of officers and strip them of their sanity.

9. QUANTIFYING THE HEROISM OF TROOPS

"Hero" is a strong word. The label of "hero" comes with a prestigious amount of respect and privilege. It's only fair that anyone who claims hero-status should have to give full account of why they deserve to hold the title of hero not just to the civilians they expect to be praised by but to the true heroes who can give full account of their hero status lest any false heroes minimize their sacrifices and accomplishments.

The current culture in America has indiscriminately lumped every member of its military into the hero category with no consideration for achievement or distinction for degrees. This is unfair to the civilian population and all true military heroes for several reasons.

Firstly, it doesn't take into account the different reasons individuals join the military. Yes, there are many individuals who enlisted because they genuinely wanted to serve their country, be all they can be and selflessly sacrifice themselves for their fellow man. These individuals' noble intentions put them in the running for hero status, and it's not fair to give mercenaries equal standing as them.

There are troops who joined the military because they were enticed by an early retirement, free education, travel opportunities, partying, a lucrative and secure paycheck, socialized healthcare for them and their family and all the other practical benefits that come along with being in the military. Some troops even joined as an alternative to prison. Anyone who joined the military for what they could get out of it is a mercenary by degrees.

Granted, they knew there was a chance of death in the line of duty, but every trucker accepts that same risk in their job to deliver goods to consumers across the nation. The big difference between a regular trucker and a mercenary is the mercenary accepts the certainty that they'll be responsible for killing other human beings (directly or indirectly). If you'd join Murder Incorporated for what you can get out of it, you've got a big task ahead of you to explain how that doesn't make you the opposite of a hero.

Regardless of why you joined the military, let's suppose you spend 20 years processing administrative paperwork in a cubicle at Lackland Air Force Base in San Antonio, Texas. Let's suppose the closest you come to a combat zone is Ali Al Salem Air Force Base in Kuwait, where you gained 10 pounds from eating steak, lobster and ice cream bars and returned home with an extra $5000 in separation and hazardous duty pay even though the closest you came to combat was playing paintball in downtown Kuwait City. Would you really tell a Marine (who has done 5 tours in Iraq and lost half his friends in combat) that you're a hero on the same level as them? No. Hell, no.

Well, if you wouldn't tell a combat infantry Marine you're just as much of a hero as them, then don't tell civilians you're a combat infantry Marine-level hero, because by my calculations processing paperwork in San Antonio for 20 years doesn't make you any more of a hero than the taxpayers who paid that Marine's paycheck.

Regardless of how close you came to the battlefield, what would happen if you refused to support the mission? Technically, the UCMJ gives the military the right to execute its own troops for going AWOL during a time of war. Granted, in this day and age the negative press that would generate almost guarantees that won't happen. What will happen though is you'll go to jail for a few months and then get kicked out of the military with no benefits... but you'll get a dishonorable discharge that's designed to almost guarantee you'll never be able to earn a living wage again for the rest of your life. This means every soldier is constantly faced with two choices: Support the mission and possibly die on the battlefield or don't support the mission and face certain destitution by your own leaders.

This means it would require as much of a sacrifice, if not more, to conscientiously object to the mission as it would to support the mission. This means it's theoretically possible to continue to support a mission you disagree with out of cowardice. This doesn't mean all troops are cowards. It just illustrates how important it is to make the distinction that not all troops are automatically heroes so as not to lump the hypocritical cowards in with the troops who do genuinely continue to serve out of courage and selflessness.

It also raises an uncomfortable point. The mere existence of the dishonorable discharge will always cast a shadow of doubt on the heroism of any soldier. I don't say that to be spiteful, at least, not to the troops. I say that to encourage discussion about whether or not the dishonorable discharge should exist at all. Is it just that the military expects civilians to embrace every troop as selfless heroes, but the military itself holds a gun to every troop's head and orders them to dance or die? Is it mentally healthy to be comfortable with this?

Some troops do willingly fight on the battlefield selflessly and die in the line of combat. Some even willingly and consciously sacrifice their lives in order to save the lives of their fellow soldiers. As taboo as it is to question the heroism of these martyrs, it's imperative to do so in order to fully validate their heroism.

Consider this. Soldiers died selflessly fighting for Hitler, Ho Chi Minh, Stalin and Pol Pot. If we made it a rule that any soldier who dies in the line of duty is automatically a hero then we owe every fallen Nazi and kamikaze pilot full hero honors on par with every American soldier who died in the Korean War, the Vietnam War or the Iraq War.

If that doesn't sound reasonable then we have to ask ourselves if reason ever played a role in our decision to call our soldiers heroes or are we really just saying that anytime one of our troops dies they become a hero and anytime anyone else's troops dies they're just the bad guy getting what they deserve? If that's what we're doing then the only determining factor in who becomes a hero is who wins the war, and that cheapens every hero's death everywhere.

Even if a man dies in battle, he still needs to pass 2 more tests before he's granted full hero status. The first question we have to ask is how their unit behaved. Did they maim or kill any civilians? Did they harass and bully civilians? Did they engage their enemy with unnecessary cruelty? Did they torture? Did they kill for sport? Did they use their victims' skulls as ashtrays? Did they commit any war crimes? Did they break the Geneva Convention?

Point in fact, there is an American War Crimes museum in Vietnam. It contains pictures of American soldiers committing war crimes. Some of those Americans in those pictures died in the line of combat and received medals. Why should they get a free pass to the hall of heroes? They wouldn't if they had Nazi flags on their shoulders instead of American flags. But the Nazis killed 6 million Jews and invaded other countries though. Well, America is responsible for the deaths of 100,000 Iraqis and has sent troops to as many, if not more countries than Germany. I'm not saying America is the same as Nazi Germany. I'm saying we need to have a measured conversation about America's military actions without whitewashing over every uncomfortable fact with euphoric propaganda.

This brings me to the second question we have to ask about our fallen soldiers before we write them into the history books as divine heroes, and that is the righteousness of the wars they fight. No matter how valiantly and selflessly any Nazi soldier fought and died, they won't be remembered as heroes by most of the world because the war they supported was unjust. The American government tells its civilians and soldiers that every war it fights is just, but every single government that has ever gone to war has always told everyone that their actions were just. Therefore, you can never take any government's reasons for going to war at face value. When a government gives you the reasons why they're going to war, that's your cue to question those reasons relentlessly....and that takes courage.

Look at the war in Iraq. Many Americans have lost their lives there. The surviving soldiers spit venom at any civilian who questions the Iraq war, but is it really the civilians who deserve to have their integrity questioned? Any American soldier who expects to be regarded as a hero or at least expects to be exempt from criticism needs to objectively analyze for themselves why America invaded Iraq.

If you look past the propaganda and look at the hard facts you'll find...nothing. George Bush claimed America had to invade Iraq because Saddam had weapons of mass destruction even though America knew Saddam didn't have nuclear capability, and the only chemical weapons Saddam had were the ones America sold him. America knew Saddam had used those weapons on civilians years before America used those war crimes as justification to hang him. When it came to light that Saddam didn't have the weapons of mass destruction General Colin Powell claimed, then George Bush changed his story and said America went into Iraq to liberate the Iraqi people. Years later, the Iraqi people still have their roads blockaded by American troops. So which reason did America go to war? Journalists, Nobel Prize winners, politicians, soldiers and citizens have been arguing for years about why America went to war in Iraq because there's no clear answer.

100,000 people dead requires a clear cut answer, which the American government has yet to produce. I can't yield unquestioning trust to a government that can't give a solid account for why it's killed so many people and spent so much of its taxpayers' hard earned money. Nor can I endorse hero status on soldiers who are killing for a cause with no clear justification. Nor can I exempt soldiers from criticism if I can't determine with certainty that the cause they serve is just. Nor should you, nor should the troops themselves.

I can't support the troops if the troops cannot give me a full account of what they're fighting for. This isn't disrespectful, arrogant, impudent or ungrateful. This is completely reasonable and justified. In response to everything said here I know that many troops (as well as family members, friends and supporters of the troops) will respond by saying, "The troops protect your freedoms...." as if that fact justifies everything they've done and exempts them from all criticism.

To this I would say, what about the Iraqi's freedom to travel? What about their freedom from search and seizure? What about their freedom from torture? America backs the Palestinian holocaust, which the rest of the world would step in and end, were it not for America's military. Even back in America, civilians don't have the freedom to marry whomever they want. Americans don't have the freedom of privacy. Our phones are wiretapped. Our genitals are groped at airports. You can't buy certain books without your name appearing on a CIA or FBI blacklist. Peace activists are put on the TSA terrorist list and lose the freedom to fly. The American government has given itself the right to take anyone in the world to secret prisons to be tortured and denied the right to a fair, public trial. Americans don't have the freedom to buy alcohol except in limited places at limited times. Americans don't have the right to grow medical marijuana.

The troops claim they protect Americans' freedoms yet America has more people in prison than any other country in the world. Americans don't have the freedom to choose how their taxes or spent. Americans don't have the freedom to dispose of a president with a 30% approval rating or a Congress with a 12% approval rating. Americans aren't protected from predatory financial practices. American women don't even have the same freedom to take off their shirt that American men have. How can you the American military supports and guarantees Americans' freedom when it's illegal for half the population to take their shirt off?

To this you might say, life is better in America than in a lot of third world countries. So Americans should be grateful and not complain. You know why life is cheap and bountiful in America? Because America actively and consistently represses the freedoms, rights and opportunities of other people so they can be used as cheap slave labor for American companies that have moved their sweatshops overseas. That's the freedom our precious military martyrs are dying for, and if you're angry at me for saying that you're directing your indignation in the wrong direction.

You can even bring the issue closer to home. The enlisted troops of the military themselves are literally slaves who are exploited and subjugated by the military caste system. The troops are made up of American civilians. Therefore the American government is enslaving civilians and justifying it by using the UCMJ as a loophole around the Universal Declaration of Human Rights. If the American government can enslave 1% of its population and systematically and brazenly brainwash those slaves to belligerently defend their own subjugation then why should I feel safe in America? The American government reserves the right to draft able-bodied men into slavery at any time as long as it claims there's a need for it, and we've seen how reliable its reasons for going to war are.

I'm not impressed by a soldier's ability to follow orders without questioning them. I'm not impressed by a soldiers' willingness to die for a cause they don't understand. I'm not impressed by the freedoms soldiers willingly surrender to men with a track record of authorizing human rights abuses and lying about it. I'm not impressed by how belligerently you tell me I'm ungrateful. I'm impressed by people who question their answers. I'm impressed by people who stand up to injustice in their own house. I'm impressed by troops who refuse to serve politicians who torture whistleblowers.

10. A VETERAN'S "STATE OF THE TROOPS" ON THE 10TH ANNIVERSARY OF SEPTEMBER 11TH

Part 1: An address to the American public

If you finish reading everything I have to say about the military and you think I'm not on the troop's side, you missed the entire point. I'll summarize my point of view by saying that the U.S. military treats the troops inhumanely. It would be considered a human rights disaster if anyone else in the world treated anyone else in the world the way governments (in particular, The United States of America) treats its military personnel. The way the U.S. military treats its troops is in violation of the universal declaration of human rights and many other laws both foreign and domestic.

The American government and the American public are complicit in these human rights abuses. The America public has quietly accepted that in order to get one person to kill another person you need to break all the rules free, civil society is based on. The American people understand that troops are systematically brainwashed, treated like 2nd class citizens and have 99% of their civil liberties, freedoms and rights voided. They know it, and they're paying all the bills to make sure it keeps happening every day.

So no America, you do not support the troops no matter how many yellow ribbon car magnets you buy. Saying you do is just insult to injury. The only reason everyone calls troops heroes is because the government has very consciously orchestrated a spectacular, highly funded charade. Without all the propaganda, all the commercials, all the pop culture references and all the memorabilia we wouldn't go along with pretending our troops are gladiators fighting for honor, glory and righteous causes in the Coliseum. We would see that our troops literally are the political equivalent of Roman gladiators who are owned, trained, lied to, systematically instilled with battered person syndrome and sent to die for the benefit of their owners under false pretenses...and when they can't be duped into marching to their death proudly they're simply forced to go against their will with a gun to their head.

On some level, we all know this, and if you don't, you do now. So now that it's been said, you have to ask yourself, what's the best way you can support the troops if there's a fraction of a chance that a fraction of this is true? I'll give you a hint. None of the following excuses help anyone:

"The troops knew what they were getting into when they signed up."

"The troops volunteered. So they can't complain."

"They took an oath. End of discussion."

"It's not for them to question why but to do and die."

If those excuses are valid then all it takes to create a second class citizen is a signature. The United States Military perpetuates the precedent that as long as you can get someone to sign a piece of paper then it's perfectly acceptable for the government to erase all the civil rights humans have fought and died for throughout human history. Think about that next time you sign a civilian job contract that waives away all your rights to any kind of legal protection from your employer no matter what they do to you or how badly you get hurt on the job as a result of their negligence. You don't have any right to complain about that because you set the precedent that paper is worth more than human life when you turned your back on the troops.

The great irony of the United States Military is that it claims to fight to protect people from being forced to live under the same conditions it forces its troops to live under. That's the irony behind your "support the troops" car magnet. You should replace it with a magnet that says, "Through hypocritical, Orwellian doublespeak, willful ignorance, flimsy excuses and apathy against the rights of my fellow human beings, I support government-sponsored brainwashing, slavery, the erosion of civilian rights and unaccountable government authority."

Part 2: An address to the American troops

The way you're being treated is tragic, and the military has put conscious effort into lying to you so that you won't see it or believe it even when it's pointed out to you. You practiced marching drills in basic training even though you never march in formation on the battlefield because marching teaches you to lose your identity in the group; it's a well-documented and time-tested brainwashing technique. So are your ranks, medals and "customs and courtesies." You take your hat off when you walk outside and put in on when you go inside as a constant reminder that every moment of your life belongs to your leaders. You're forced to call your "superiors" "sir" and "ma'am" as a constant reminder that your will is worth less than theirs. A true leader, someone worth following, would never say, "Salute me out of respect or I'll send you to jail and end your career." A leader worth following would never tell you, "It's not for you to question why but to do and die." Only an abusive manipulator would say that to another human being. We were all born equal. Every breath we take, we take as equals, and we'll die as equals. Anyone who tells you differently is not your friend and not worthy of respect.

I understand that many troops volunteered for pure, selfless, heroic reasons. Even the troops whose primary motive in signing up was a steady paycheck, I understand that you sleep well at night believing that, incidentally, you support truth, justice, freedom and peace. I understand that if it came down to it, most of you would literally, willingly step in front of a bullet for the sake of the civilian population. I can't thank you enough for the sentiment.

The thing about that is, what you're doing right now is accomplishing the opposite of what your leaders promised you it would. They know that. That's why they won't allow you to question them. It's not because there's no time to explain. It's not because global politics are too hard for you to understand. It's not because there's anything truly heroic about not thinking for yourself. It's certainly not because your leaders are so righteous that questioning their integrity or intelligence would be an exercise in futility. You're told not to exercise or trust your own ability to reason because the more you do that, the more likely you'll come to the logical realization that your leadership has systematically constructed an elaborate bubble around you and is lying to you to get you to do someone else's dirty work that violates your strict code of ethics and honor. While you're busying hating me for saying this, your leadership is laughing at you all the way to the bank.

I know I'm attacking all the beliefs you hold dear, but you have to see that I'm doing it because my heart bleeds for the troops. Having said that, I have one more hard thing to say. You don't have any excuse for supporting an unjust war. Not at this point.

I was an Airman First Class stationed in Aviano, Italy on September 11th, 2001. That day we went into Threatcon Delta and scrambled our fighter jets not knowing which direction to look for the next incoming attack. We were scared and confused, but we did our jobs and we didn't ask questions because there wasn't time for second guessing. Not long after that our flight line was full of C-130s sending troops to Northern Iraq. We didn't fully understand why we were sending troops to Iraq, but our president promised us that we were the good guys, the terrorists hated our freedoms, Saddam had WMDs and he posed an imminent threat to the American public. I was skeptical until General Colin Powell explained the whole situation in detail with pictures. Then, even though I couldn't turn a corner in Italy without seeing fifty "Pace" (Peace) flags insinuating I was a monster, I had faith in our leaders. So I did my job and slept soundly.

It's been ten years now, and the verdict is in. The WMDs were a lie. Iraq had nothing to do with September 11th. Saddam Hussein was never even a remote threat to the American people. The only WMDs he had, he bought from America. Since Saddam was removed from power more Iraqis have died as a result of America's actions than Saddam Hussein's did or could have. The Iraqi people want America out of their country. The American occupation in the Middle East isn't protecting anyone's freedoms, and it's not making the world safe from terrorism. The American occupation in the Middle East has created living conditions in those countries worth fighting against. It's scary there, and it's making people hate America who otherwise wouldn't have. The actions of the American military are creating terrorists and bankrupting America.

That's just what the American military is actively doing. The other, less publicized side of the coin is what the American military is passively preventing from happening. Palestinians are living in Holocaust-conditions. They're being ethnically cleansed. Boats full of aid workers trying to reach the victims are being shot at and blockaded by Israel. Yet the world stands by and watches in horror because every nation in the world knows that if they step in to help then America will turn its gargantuan, unquestioning military on them.

The world economy is strangled in economic policies and embargoes held in place by the threat of American military "intervention." All the while murderous dictators are given free rein to step on the rights and lives of their people as long as they play ball with America. Threat of American military intervention keeps millions (if not billions) of people trapped in poverty, misery, fear, despair, indignity and danger every day.

These aren't conspiracy theories. These claims consistently make front page news, not just in the mainstream, left-wing, American media but in every major media outlet around the entire globe. Everyone is talking about it everywhere. Hundreds, if not thousands of books have been written about it, and world leaders weigh it in their decisions every day. The world practically revolves around it. This means that the American troops no longer have the luxury of feigning ignorance by saying, "I was just following orders." "I trust my leaders." "I was just doing my duty." "It's not my place to question." "There's no time to ask questions." "The verdict is still out." No. The verdict is in. I'm sorry, but you're not acting like good guys even if the intention is there.

Your duty to your current employer doesn't supersede your duty to humanity no matter what oaths they handed you to recite. It's your responsibility to question your actions. When someone tells you to kill someone else, the only correct response is, "I'm going to research this issue to the core of the onion and second guess myself right up to the last moment." That's called holding yourself accountable, and that's a cornerstone of maturity. Suicidal servitude is not.

It's not like you're going to have to do some deep, dark soul searching to even face the possibility that the official Disney version of recent history as told by the United States Military Public Affairs Office is bullshit. In fact, I wouldn't believe any troop who says the idea never occurred to them. I expect most troops understand this truth better than most civilians. I know that 70% of the conversations that take place in military smoke pits every day are about how much the military sucks and how it cuts its own throat with its broken, outdated, backward bureaucracy. The troops know better than anyone that military bureaucracy is a wasteful menace kept afloat because it's such a lucrative cash cow. On some level, all the troops know this is true. The question is, when will you fully admit that the giant, bloody elephant in the room that everyone (even you) is talking about is real?

As long as that bloody elephant stays in the room you don't have the right to sleep well at night. Don't get mad at me for pointing out the obvious. Get mad at your leadership for misleading you and putting you in that position. And don't tell me, "I don't agree with you, but thanks to my sacrifices you have the luxury to say those ignorant, disgusting things." No. your sacrifices have not secured my freedoms in any way. In fact, the citizens you claim to be protecting have lost significant freedoms, liberties and dignities on your watch. And you know who took those freedoms from the people you were supposed to be protecting. Your leaders did. I'm afraid to even bring it up in public, because I'm afraid of those leaders and the unquestioning military force they control. I accept that I'm probably on a no-fly list despite (or because of) the fact that I'm a very vocal advocate of freedom, equality and nonviolence. I haven't tested that theory because I have too much pride to fly and allow myself to be violated by the TSA. So, no. You don't get to dismiss any criticism of the military, its leaders or its personnel by claiming to fight for anyone's freedoms. I wish you could, but your leaders took that card away from you.

When I was enlisted I didn't have the courage to consciously object and go to jail for standing up for truth, justice and freedom. I wish I had so I could ask the same of you today. I understand your fear of your employer. So I urge you, don't reenlist. Get out as soon as possible. Talk others out of joining. Starve the military industrial war complex of its slaves and make the world a safer place for everyone.

11. AN OPEN LETTER TO THE UNITED STATES MILITARY

Dear Active Duty Troops,

Take another look at the oath you swore at MEPS:

"I, _____, do solemnly swear (or affirm) that I will support and defend the Constitution of the United States against all enemies, foreign and domestic; that I will bear true faith and allegiance to the same; and that I will obey the orders of the President of the United States and the orders of the officers appointed over me, according to regulations and the Uniform Code of Military Justice. So help me God."

Did you ever notice that nowhere in that oath does it say anything about the well-being of the American people? The closest it comes is citing a secondary source: The U.S. Constitution, which gives a nod to the people, but the U.S. Constitution is also the legal document that politicians base their powers on... politicians who have given themselves the power to tag anyone, even Americans as a terrorist with no accountability. So this oath swears loyalty to politicians who don't honor any parts of the Constitution except the parts that give them power.

The enlistment oath also swears unquestioning allegiance to the Uniform Code of Military Justice (UCMJ), a legal document written by politicians that violate the Constitution and the Universal Declaration of Human Rights by outlining and legitimizing the operation of the world's largest, oldest death cult. I don't say that as an insult. I'm objectively pointing at the writing on the wall. The UCMJ took everything psychologists know about the dark side of modern psychology and designed the world's most professional, streamlined cult. Before the civil rights movement of the mid-1900s this wasn't a big deal, but once enough precedents had been set that people have to be treated humanely the military simply side-stepped that responsibility by creating the UCMJ.

This is an unflattering critique of the U.S. military's most sacred document, but the math adds up. It's all right there in plain sight. Look it up. Or you can enlist and see for yourself or get a job as a civilian contractor for the military and see the outcome first hand. The field slaves answer to the house slaves, and the house slaves answer to the politicians. If you've ever watched the news or turned on the internet then you should be able to connect the rest of the dots yourself. The politicians answer to their campaign donors, and their campaign donors are the 1%. So the United States military is a death cult directly and solely accountable to the highest bidder. That's not a conspiracy. That's a paper trail the size of the Grand Canyon.

What does the highest bidder want? The highest bidder wants the politicians who represent them to control more of anything and everything in the world that will make them more money. One of the things that make the rich richest, is selling weapons and support to the military. War profiteers are making money hand over fist from both ends of the military, and the more money they make, the more certain they can make it that the only thing that will ever change is they'll get richer...by waging more wars whether the world needs them or not. That and photo ops is what the United States Military was designed to stand for, and that explains every major military conflict America has been in since WWII much better than the overgeneralized-to-the-point-of-being-useless explanations the U.S. military's public affairs department puts on its press releases.

That much alone should warrant a deafening public outcry for military reform and a boycott of reenlistments, but the situation is more dire than that. Not that the oath of enlistment directly mentions protecting civilians, but any active duty troop who felt in their heart that their oath was to protect the rights, freedoms and dignities of the American civilian population, has failed. The American people got sold out on the troops' watch.

The troops fail every day a TSA agent touches a person's genitals. The troops fail every time the government eavesdrops on citizens. The troops fail every time the police incarcerate another drug addict. The troops fail every time an American can't see a doctor. The troops fail every time poisonous additives are added to the food sold in grocery stores. The troops fail every time a university raises tuition. The troops fail every time workers lose the right to form unions. The troops fail every time a presidential candidate is caught telling a lie. The troops fail every time an officer orders an enlisted soldier to choose between saluting them or going to jail. Every troop fails every time a single troop tortures a prisoner of war.

On a wider scale, the troops fail every day the North Korean dynasty stays in power. The troops fail every time an Israeli soldier burns a Palestinian's olive grove. The troops fail every time an African warlord rapes a child. The troops fail every time America's political sanctions kill a child. The troops fail every time a drone kills an innocent person. The richer the rich get and the poorer the poor get the more the troops fail. For all the little signs of hope you see in the war zones you've created, the rest of the world is crumbling as a direct result of your actions and inactions.

The call to action isn't for people to spit on troops. Troops aren't villains, they're victims. The call to action is for everyone to read the UCMJ. If you can't understand it, go through it line by line with a lawyer, a psychologist and a cult leader. They can point out the sinister parts. Then talk to others about the need to reform the UCMJ. It took decades of everyone inside and out of the military screaming that gays should be able to enlist before the wheels of the military bureaucracy creaked around to allowing it. It's going to take more talk than that to bring the entire UCMJ into compliance with the U.S. Constitution and the Declaration of Human Rights let alone pull the linchpin that connects military power to corporate profits.

Ignorance and silence are all the highest bidders need to keep big war profitable. Study the UCMJ and the U.S. military in general. If it has real flaws, the solution isn't to take offense when they're brought up. If you eat, sleep and breath military then your patriotism should motivate you to find and address the flaws in the military yourself, because as it stands, your leaders are undermining your oath. If you're not in the military, and you live in fear of the U.S. military and/or the corporate interests it serves, then study the UCMJ and the industrial military war complex and find a way to peacefully and respectfully let it be known that the UCMJ doesn't meet the needs or moral standards of your generation.

Sincerely,

A troop who stopped drinking the Kool-Aid

www.ingramcontent.com/pod-product-compliance
Lightning Source LLC
Chambersburg PA
CBHW020928180526
45163CB00007B/2922